Level **1**

4th Edition

Listening & **Notetaking** Skills

Patricia A. Dunkel & Phyllis L. Lim

With

Christine Salica Seal

Australia • Brazil • Japan • Korea • Mexico • Singapore • Spain • United Kingdom • United States

Listening and Notetaking Skills 1:
Intermediate Listening Comprehension,
Fourth Edition

Patricia A. Dunkel and Phyllis L. Lim

Publisher: Sherrise Roehr

Executive Editor: Laura Le Dréan

Director of Global Marketing: Ian Martin

International Marketing Manager: Caitlin Thomas

Product Manager: Emily Stewart

Director, Content and Media Production:
Michael Burggren

Content Project Manager: Andrea Bobotas

Print Buyer: Mary Beth Hennebury

Cover Designers: Christopher Roy and
Michael Rosenquest

Cover Image: Frans Lanting/National Geographic
Stock

Compositor: Page Designs International

For product information and technology assistance, contact us at
Cengage Learning Customer & Sales Support,
1-800-354-9706

For permission to use material from this text or product,
submit all requests online at **www.cengage.com/permissions**.
Further permissions questions can be e-mailed to
permissionrequest@cengage.com.

Student Book ISBN: 978-1-133-95114-8

National Geographic Learning
20 Channel Center Street
Boston, MA 02210
USA

Cengage Learning is a leading provider of customized learning solutions with office locations around the globe, including Singapore, the United Kingdom, Australia, Mexico, Brazil and Japan.

Cengage Learning products are represented in Canada by Nelson Education, Ltd.

Visit National Geographic Learning online at **ngl.cengage.com**

Visit our corporate website at **www.cengage.com**

Printed in the United States of America
1 2 3 4 5 6 7 8 9 10   15 14 13

CONTENTS

Scope and Sequence   iv

Unit Walkthrough   vi

UNIT 1   **Chronology:** Talking about When Things Happen   1

    Chapter 1   **Napoleon:** From Schoolboy to Emperor   2

    Chapter 2   **Pompeii:** Destroyed, Forgotten, and Found   9

    Chapter 3   **Steve Jobs:** A Man with a Vision   16

    Video   **Surviving an Avalanche**   22

UNIT 2   **Process:** Describing How Things Work   25

    Chapter 4   **Roller Coasters:** The Ups and Downs of How They Work   26

    Chapter 5   **Language:** How Children Acquire Theirs   33

    Chapter 6   **Robots:** How They Work and Learn to Work   39

    Video   **Tristan da Cunha Oil Spill**   46

UNIT 3   **Classification:** Defining and Putting Things into Categories   49

    Chapter 7   **A Tidal Wave:** What Is It? Can We Predict It?   50

    Chapter 8   **Levels of Language:** Formal and Informal   56

    Chapter 9   **Power:** The Kinds of Power People Use and Abuse   63

    Video   **People, Plants, and Pollinators**   70

UNIT 4   **Comparison and Contrast:** Describing Similarities and Differences   73

    Chapter 10   **Asian and African Elephants:** Similarities and Differences   74

    Chapter 11   **Lincoln and Kennedy:** Different Times, Similar Destinies   81

    Chapter 12   **The *Titanic* and the *Costa Concordia*:** Tragedies at Sea   88

    Video   **Free Soloing with Alex Honnold**   94

UNIT 5   **Cause and Effect:** Describing the Reason Things Happen   97

    Chapter 13   **Dinosaurs:** Why They Disappeared   98

    Chapter 14   **The U.S. Civil War:** Why It Happened   105

    Chapter 15   **Endangered Species:** Why Are They Endangered?   112

    Video   **The Surma People**   118

Appendix A   Audioscripts   121

Appendix B   Videoscripts   163

Credits   166

SCOPE AND SEQUENCE

	Unit		Chapter

1 **Chronology**
Talking about When Things Happen

1 **Napoleon**
From Schoolboy to Emperor

2 **Pompeii**
Destroyed, Forgotten, and Found

3 **Steve Jobs**
A Man with a Vision

2 **Process**
Describing How Things Work

4 **Roller Coasters**
The Ups and Downs of How They Work

5 **Language**
How Children Acquire Theirs

6 **Robots**
How They Work and Learn to Work

3 **Classification**
Defining and Putting Things into Categories

7 **A Tidal Wave**
What Is It? Can We Predict It?

8 **Levels of Language**
Formal and Informal

9 **Power**
The Kinds of Power People Use and Abuse

4 **Comparison and Contrast**
Describing Similarities and Differences

10 **Asian and African Elephants**
Similarities and Differences

11 **Lincoln and Kennedy**
Different Times, Similar Destinies

12 **The *Titanic* and the *Costa Concordia***
Tragedies at Sea

5 **Cause and Effect**
Describing the Reason Things Happen

13 **Dinosaurs**
Why They Disappeared

14 **The U.S. Civil War**
Why It Happened

15 **Endangered Species**
Why Are They Endangered?

Notetaking Preparation	Expansion	Unit Video

- Notetaking Basics: Abbreviations and Symbols

Task 1: Famous Historical Figures
Task 2: The History of the Bicycle

Surviving an Avalanche

- Using Symbols in Notes

Task 1: What Happened First?
Task 2: Famous Volcanoes of the World

- Time Lines

Task 1: The Evolution of the Computer
Task 2: Landmarks in Technology

- Steps in a Process

Task 1: Taking a Pulse
Task 2: Yoga Poses

Tristan da Cunha Oil Spill

- Abbreviating Frequently Repeated Words

Task 1: Stages in Language Development
Task 2: Writing an E-mail

- Listening for New Sections of a Lecture

Task 1: Steps in Doing Research
Task 2: A Simple Experiment

- Recording Definitions

Task 1: Listening for Definitions
Task 2: Natural Disasters

People, Plants, and Pollinators

- Listening for Examples

Task 1: Homonyms and Homophones
Task 2: Classifying Parts of Speech

- Listening for Classifying Language

Task 1: Classifying Animals
Task 2: What's That Animal?

- Making a Comparison Chart

Task 1: The Hippo and the Rhino
Task 2: Two Brothers

Free Soloing with Alex Honnold

- Listening to the Lecture Overview

Task 1: Two First Ladies
Task 2: Two Vice Presidents

- Making Your Notes Complete

Task 1: The Hindenburg Disaster
Task 2: Easily Confused Words

- Using Arrows for Cause and Effect

Task 1: What's the Reason?
Task 2: You Write the Ending

The Surma People

- When Not to Take Notes

Task 1: The Revolutionary War
Task 2: Guessing Causes

- Listening for a Review of the Lecture

Task 1: Endangered Species
Task 2: Types of Pollution

UNIT WALKTHROUGH

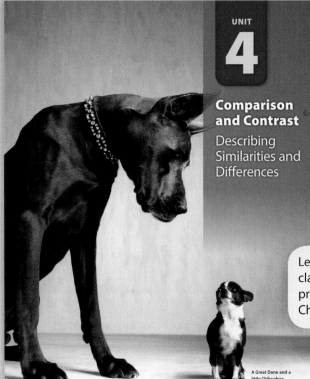

UNIT

4

Comparison and Contrast
Describing Similarities and Differences

A Great Dane and a little Chihuahua

New to This Edition

- Authentic **National Geographic videos** provide a meaningful context for discussion and application of essential listening, notetaking, and vocabulary skills.

- New and updated **academic lectures** offer compelling, cross-curricular content that simulate authentic scenarios for maximum academic readiness.

- Every unit introduces a focused aspect of **notetaking** and provides varied opportunities for practice and application of the skill.

Learners prepare for notetaking in the academic classroom through focused instruction and practice on organizational modes such as Chronology, Process, and Cause and Effect.

Before Listening activities prepare students for success by activating background knowledge and providing the language and skills necessary for comprehension.

CHAPTER

10

Asian and African Elephants
Similarities and Differences

A young elephant in Kaziranga National Park, India

TOPIC PREVIEW

Answer the following questions with a partner or your classmates.

1. Discuss the animals you see in the photo on this page. What do you know about these animals?

2. Have you ever seen a real elephant? Describe where and when you saw it. What impressed you most about the animal?

3. Talk about the similarities and differences between elephants (the largest animals that live on land) and whales (the largest animals that live in water).

VOCABULARY PREVIEW

(CD 5, TR 1) **A** Listen to the following sentences that contain information from the lecture. As you listen, write the word from the box that completes the sentence.

enormous	fascinating	mammals	tamer	temperament
trained	trunk	tusks	wilder	

1. Today's topic is the largest land _____ on earth—elephants.

2. Elephants are _____ animals.

3. An elephant uses its _____ to put grasses, leaves, and water into its mouth.

4. Elephants can be _____ to do heavy work.

5. The Asian elephant sometimes does not have any _____ at all.

6. A big difference between the two types of elephants is their _____.

7. The Asian elephant is _____ than the African elephant.

8. The African elephant is much _____ than the Asian elephant.

9. There certainly are differences between the African and the Asian elephants, but they are both _____ animals.

B Match the words to their definitions.

_____ 1. mammal   a. the long nose of an elephant

_____ 2. enormous   b. to teach to do something

_____ 3. fascinating   c. easy for people to control and teach

_____ 4. tame   d. one of the two long teeth that an elephant has

_____ 5. temperament e. very difficult for people to control

_____ 6. train   f. of very great or large size; huge

_____ 7. trunk   g. very interesting

_____ 8. tusk   h. nature; outlook; personality

_____ 9. wild   i. an animal that feeds its own milk to its babies

PREDICTIONS

Think about the questions in the Topic Preview on page 74 and the sentences you heard in the Vocabulary Preview. Write three questions that you think will be answered in the lecture. Share your questions with your classmates.

The *Notetaking Preparation* section presents a variety of effective notetaking techniques. Using content from the unit, students practice these techniques in authentic academic situations.

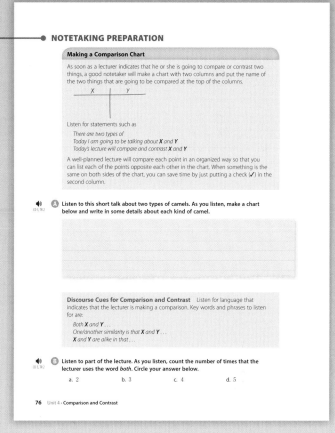

Making a Comparison Chart

As soon as a lecturer indicates that he or she is going to compare or contrast two things, a good notetaker will make a chart with two columns and put the name of the two things that are going to be compared at the top of the columns.

Listen for statements such as

There are two types of
Today I am going to be talking about X and Y
Today's lecture will compare and contrast X and Y

A well-planned lecture will compare each point in an organized way so that you can list each of the points opposite each other in the chart. When something is the same on both sides of the chart, you can save time by just putting a check (✓) in the second column.

🔊 **A** Listen to this short talk about two types of camels. As you listen, make a chart below and write in some details about each kind of camel.

Discourse Cues for Comparison and Contrast Listen for language that indicates that the lecturer is making a comparison. Key words and phrases to listen for are:

Both X and Y . . .
One/another similarity is that X and Y . . .
X and Y are alike in that . . .

🔊 **B** Listen to part of the lecture. As you listen, count the number of times that the lecturer uses the word *both*. Circle your answer below.

a. 2   b. 3   c. 4   d. 5

76 Unit 4 · Comparison and Contrast

Notetaking Skills

Throughout the *Listening & Notetaking Skills* series, learners develop a wide variety of notetaking strategies necessary for academic success. Learners are taught the essential principles of notetaking and encouraged to personalize the strategies for maximum results.

LISTENING

🔊 **FIRST LISTENING**

Listen to the lecture on elephants. As you listen, put the following parts of the lecture in the order that you hear them. Number them 1 to 5.

_____ The continents elephants come from

_____ Elephants' temperaments

_____ Elephants' trunks

_____ Elephants' size

_____ Elephants' intelligence

🔊 **SECOND LISTENING**

Listen to information from the lecture. The speaker will talk slowly and carefully. You don't have to do anything as you listen. Just relax and listen.

THIRD LISTENING

Listen to the lecture in two parts. Follow the directions for each part. When you have finished, review your notes. Later, you will use them to summarize the lecture with a partner.

🔊 Part 1

You will hear the first part of the lecture again. Listen and complete the notes by adding the abbreviations and symbols from the box.

| ✓ | e.g. | gals | + | Afr. |

Asian E	_____ E
has trunk	✓
eats leaves + grass	
picks up obj _____ trees	
drinks 50 _____ H₂O per day	_____
intellgnt	✓
heavy work	
do tricks _____ entertain	

🔊 Part 2

As you listen to the second part of the lecture, take your own notes on a separate piece of paper.

Listening sections introduce the academic lecture. Learners listen to the lecture three times, focusing on a different listening and notetaking skill with each repetition.

Chapter 10 · Asian and African Elephants **77**

After Listening sections provide learners with opportunities to discuss the lecture through pair and group activities.

The Oral Summary asks learners to use their notes to reconstruct the content of the lecture.

Through guided prompts, Discussion activities provide opportunities for learners to hone communicative and critical thinking skills.

The Expansion section in each chapter provides opportunities for learners to broaden their knowledge of the featured rhetorical mode through a variety of listening and critical thinking activities.

AFTER LISTENING

ACCURACY CHECK

(A) You will hear four questions about the lecture. Listen to each question and write the letter of the best answer.

_____ 1. a. ear
b. trunk
c. tooth
d. tusk

_____ 2. a. African elephants
b. Asian elephants
c. both Asian and African
d. neither African nor Asian

_____ 3. a. 7,000 to 12,000 lbs.
b. 8,000 to 10,000 lbs.
c. 12,000 to 14,000 lbs.
d. 18,000 to 20,000 lbs.

_____ 4. a. larger and lighter
b. heavier and larger
c. lighter and smaller
d. smaller and heavier

(B) You will hear five statements about the lecture. Listen to each statement and decide if you heard the information in the lecture. Write Y for yes or N for no.

1. _____   2. _____   3. _____   4. _____   5. _____

ORAL SUMMARY

Use your notes to create an oral summary of the lecture with your partner. As you work together, add details to your notes that your partner included but you had missed.

DISCUSSION

Discuss the following questions with a classmate or in a small group.

1. Some people say the one animal that doesn't belong in a zoo is the elephant. Do you agree? Why? Do you think there are animals other than elephants that don't belong in zoos or circuses?

2. Compare two domestic animals (dog, cat, horse, etc.) and two wild animals (giraffe, bear, wolf, etc.). How are the two domestic animals similar and different? How are the two wild animals similar and different?

3. Some Asian elephants are working animals that are trained to do work such as lifting tree trunks for people. What animals do work in your country? What work do they do?

4. How are the kinds of pets sold in pet stores and those given away by animal rescue organizations such as the ASPCA similar or different?

EXPANSION

TASK 1 The Hippo and the Rhino

(A) Listen to the talk about the similarities and differences between the hippopotamus—the hippo—and the rhinoceros—the rhino. As you listen, complete the Venn diagram with the information below.

herbivores		loners		very big and heavy
have horns				
endangered		eat at night	social animals	can be found in Asia
good swimmers		can be found in Africa		

Hippos   Rhinos

(B) Compare your answers with a partner and make sentences that compare and contrast the two animals.

TASK 2 Two Brothers

(A) Listen for similarities and differences between two brothers, Charlie and David. As you listen, put a check (✓) in the correct box under each picture.

Charlie		David
☐	is married	☐
☐	has two children	☐
☐	has a girl and a boy	☐
☐	works in an office	☐
☐	works as a firefighter	☐
☐	likes jazz music	☐
☐	likes to play golf	☐
☐	is wealthy	☐

(B) Compare your answers with a partner.

Unit Video

Each unit ends with an authentic **National Geographic** video that is related to the unit theme. Most of the videos are in a lecture format, giving students a further opportunity to practice notetaking skills.

UNIT 4
VIDEO

Free Soloing with Alex Honnold

B Work with a partner and discuss answers to the following questions.

1. Is there anything that is **well within your ability** to do but not easy for other people that you know?
2. Does your life **revolve around** a particular person, place, or activity?
3. In what areas can some people be **unbelievably gifted**?
4. What special **gear** do you need to do an activity that you enjoy doing?
5. Describe a time when you decided to stop doing something and to **switch** and do something different.
6. At what age do you think you were **at the top of your game**?
7. What experiences have you had that you would describe as "**awesome**" or "**memorable moments**"?

BEFORE VIEWING

TOPIC PREVIEW

Work with a partner to make a list or draw pictures in the box below. Draw or list the different pieces of equipment mountain climbers use to keep them safe when they climb.

VOCABULARY PREVIEW

A Read the definitions of these key words and phrases that you will hear during the video.

gear special equipment used to do a particular activity or sport
at the top of [this] game at the very highest level of ability
unbelievably gifted with an amazing, incredible natural talent
revolves around turns in a circle about a central point that is the focus
memorable moments times that are so enjoyable or important in your life that you expect you will always remember them
switched changed
well within his ability something that he could easily do
awesome amazing, extraordinary, fantastic, wonderful

VIEWING

FIRST VIEWING

Watch the video, and then compare your first impressions with a partner. Talk about what you remember, what surprised you, and what interested you.

SECOND VIEWING

Watch the video again. Listen for the missing words and write them in the blanks.

1. Free soloing has to be the ultimate in free _____.
2. The reason it's probably the ultimate is because one _____ move, you fall, you die.
3. Yeah, I would say that Yosemite probably is the _____ of my climbing.
4. For most people on this planet who are serious climbers, doing Half Dome in a day or two is considered _____. Alex did it in three hours, without a _____.
5. I've sort of embraced the whole _____, you know, embraced the unpleasant parts, too.

Half Dome, Yosemite National Park

Listening and Notetaking Skills Series Components

The Audio CDs provide all the lectures and listening activities contained in the Student Book.

The Video DVD contains five authentic **National Geographic** videos relating to the units in the book.

Chronology

Talking about When Things Happen

Photographs of an eclipse taken at five-minute intervals

Napoleon

From Schoolboy to Emperor

TOPIC PREVIEW

Answer the following questions with a partner or your classmates.

1. Who was Napoleon Bonaparte? What is he famous for?

2. When do you think Napoleon was born?

3. How are Alexander the Great, Julius Caesar, and George Washington like Napoleon? Do you know any dates of the important events in these people's lives?

Napoleon Bonaparte

VOCABULARY PREVIEW

CD 1, TR 1

A Listen to the following sentences that contain information from the lecture. As you listen, write the word from the box that completes the sentence.

campaign	controlled	deserted	emperor
excelled	fame	figures	victories

1. One of the most important historical _____ in European history was Napoleon Bonaparte.

2. Napoleon _____ in mathematics and military science.

3. In 1785, Napoleon began the military career that brought him _____, power, riches, and, finally, defeat.

4. Napoleon won many _____ on the battlefield.

5. Napoleon became the first _____ of France.

6. At one time, Napoleon _____ most of Europe.

7. In his military _____ against Russia, Napoleon lost most of his army.

8. The great French conqueror died alone, _____ by his family and friends.

B Match the words to their definitions.

_____ 1. desert

_____ 2. fame

_____ 3. control

_____ 4. victory

_____ 5. emperor

_____ 6. campaign

_____ 7. figure

_____ 8. excel

a. a planned series of actions against an enemy

b. to leave all alone

c. the recognition of many people for something you did

d. a person, usually someone important in a particular way

e. success in winning a competition or war

f. to have power or authority over something

g. to do extremely well

h. the ruler of a group of countries

PREDICTIONS

Think about the questions in the Topic Preview on page 2 and the sentences you heard in the Vocabulary Preview. Write three questions that you think will be answered in the lecture. Share your questions with your classmates.

NOTETAKING PREPARATION

Notetaking Basics: Abbreviations and Symbols

When you listen to a lecture and take notes, you have to write down a lot of information very quickly. Don't try to write every word. Use symbols and abbreviations as much as possible.

■ Abbreviate names, places, and titles by using the first letter or the first several letters. You can use a period, but when taking notes, this isn't always necessary.

R. (Rita)	S. (Steve)	US (United States)
S.A. (South America)	Prof (Professor)	Gen (General)
Pres (President)	dir. (director)	

■ Abbreviate important words in a lecture by shortening them.

exc (excelled)	milit sch (military school)
fath (father)	bril (brilliant)

■ Use symbols to indicate relationships between things.

& (and)	= (equals, is, has)
≠ (not, not the same as)	@ (at)

CD 1, TR 2

A Listen to information from the lecture. Match the notes below to the information you hear. Write the number of the sentence in the blank.

_____ N. = exc math & milit sc

_____ @ 16 Fr. arm

_____ N. ≠ gd stud

_____ att Rus. & defeated

_____ N. died 1821 @ 51

Discourse Cues for Chronology In a lecture with historical information, listen for dates. In English, when a year is given, the speaker will first give the number for the century, for example, *eighteen*; and then the number within the century, for example, *twenty-three*. So 1823 is said, *eighteen twenty-three*. When the year is in the first decade of the century, however, the speaker will say, *O five, O six, O seven*, and so on. So 1902 is said, *nineteen O two*.

CD 1, TR 2

B Listen to four dates. As you listen, write the dates as numbers in the spaces below.

1. _____   3. _____

2. _____   4. _____

FIRST LISTENING

CD 1, TR 3

Listen to the lecture about Napoleon. As you listen, put the following parts of the lecture in the order that you hear them. Number them 1 to 5.

_____ Napoleon is all alone.

_____ Napoleon controls most of Europe.

_____ Napoleon lives on Corsica.

_____ Napoleon becomes Emperor of France.

_____ Napoleon attacks Russia.

SECOND LISTENING

CD 1, TR 4

Listen to information from the lecture. The speaker will talk slowly and carefully. You don't have to do anything as you listen. Just relax and listen.

THIRD LISTENING

Listen to the lecture in two parts. Follow the directions for each part. When you have finished, review your notes. Later, you will use them to summarize the lecture with a partner.

Part 1

CD 1, TR 5

You will hear the first part of the lecture again. Listen and complete the notes by adding the abbreviations and symbols from the box.

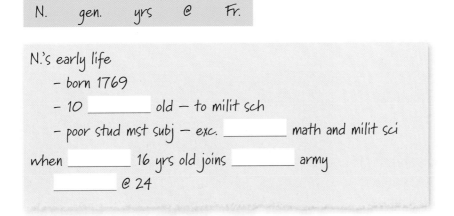

N.	gen.	yrs	@	Fr.

N.'s early life
- born 1769
- 10 _____ old — to milit sch
- poor stud mst subj — exc. _____ math and milit sci
when _____ 16 yrs old joins _____ army
_____ @ 24

Part 2

CD 1, TR 5

As you listen to the second part of the lecture, take your own notes on a separate piece of paper.

🔊 ACCURACY CHECK

CD 1, TR 6

You will hear questions and statements about the lecture. For 1–4, listen to the question and write the letter of the best answer. For 5–8, listen to the statement and write *T* for *true* or *F* for *false*.

_____ 1. a. in 1821
b. in France
c. in 1769
d. in Corsica

_____ 2. a. outstanding
b. excellent
c. good
d. poor

_____ 3. a. power
b. wealth
c. defeat
d. all of the above

_____ 4. a. when he was 51 years old
b. in 1804
c. after he attacked Russia
d. just before he defeated England

5. _____   6. _____   7. _____   8. _____

ORAL SUMMARY

Use your notes to create an oral summary of the lecture with your partner. As you work together, add details to your notes that your partner included but you had missed.

DISCUSSION

Discuss the following statements with a classmate or in a small group.

1. Napoleon was a great man.

2. It would be impossible today for a person to have a career like Napoleon's.

3. Ten-year-old children are too young to be sent to a military school.

4. Every young man and woman should be required to do at least two years of military service for his or her country.

TASK 1 Famous Historical Figures

A Listen to six short biographies of famous figures in history. As you listen, fill in the missing information in the sentences below. The first one is done for you.

CD 1, TR 7

1. I lived in Central _____Asia_____. I ruled a large empire. I am Genghis Kahn, born in _____1167_____.

2. I am _____ the Great. I became ruler of my people in _____ BCE.

3. In _____ I traveled to China. I am from _____. My name is Marco Polo.

4. I am Suleiman the Magnificent. I ruled the _____ Empire from the year _____.

5. I am from _____. I was a great queen who died at age 39 in _____ BCE.

6. My name brings fear to many. I was born around the year _____. In _____ I conquered Gaul. I am _____ the Hun.

B Work with a partner and complete the time line below. Use information from the sentences in **A** above. The first one is done for you.

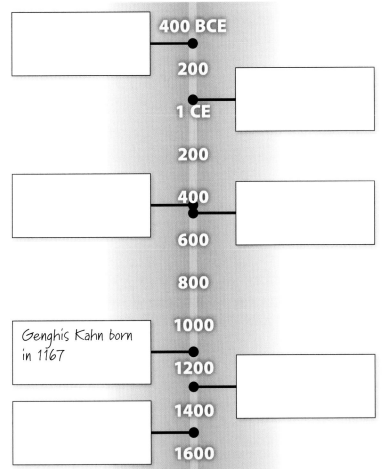

Time line:
- 400 BCE
- 200
- 1 CE
- 200
- 400
- 600
- 800
- 1000
- 1200
- 1400
- 1600
- 1800

Genghis Kahn born in 1167

Statue of Genghis Kahn

TASK 2 The History of the Bicycle

CD 1, TR 8

A Listen to a short history of the bicycle. As you listen and read, write the missing information in the blank spaces. The first one is done for you.

History of the Bicycle

The earliest "bicycle" appeared in France in the _____1790s_____. It was a little
wooden horse with a front wheel that could not be turned right or left. This little horse did
not have any pedals, and the only way it could be moved was by the rider pushing against
the ground with his or her feet.

In _____, the German baron Karl von Drais made a front wheel that
could turn. Now the rider could direct the wooden horse right or left. The rider still needed
to push it with his or her feet on the ground.

The next development occurred in _____, when a Scottish blacksmith,
Kirkpatrick MacMillan, designed the first bicyclelike machine with pedals. MacMillan rode
his machine the 70 miles from his home to Glasgow, Scotland, in only _____.

In _____ Pierre Lallement applied for and received a U.S. patent for a
machine that he called the "bisicle." Some people called it a "boneshaker" because it had
steel wheels. _____ later, in 1869, rubber tires were introduced
and the bicycle got more comfortable. Around the same time, the
front wheels began to get larger and the back wheels got smaller.

The first "highwheeler" was introduced in 1872. During the
_____, bicycles enjoyed a sudden growth in
popularity. The highwheelers were very popular, especially
among young men. They could go very fast, but they weren't
very safe. A rider sitting high up on the bicycle and traveling
very fast could easily fall off if the bicycle hit even a small
bump in the road.

Fortunately, the "safety bicycle" was invented in
_____. The safety bicycle had equal-sized wheels, a
chain, and a gear-driven rear wheel. The rider was now sitting further back on the bicycle
and in less danger. More improvements followed. Pneumatic tires—that is, tires with air in
them—were invented in _____. The last major innovation, the derailleur gear,
arrived _____ after that, in 1899.

Beginning in the _____, bicycles became lighter, and changes in design
and materials allowed bicycles to go faster. No doubt there will be more improvements in
design and materials in the future.

B Check your answers with a partner.

Pompeii

Destroyed, Forgotten, and Found

TOPIC PREVIEW

Answer the following questions with a partner or your classmates.

1. Where is the city of Pompeii? What natural disaster happened there about 2,000 years ago?

2. Have you or someone you know ever experienced a natural disaster? What happened?

3. Name one or two cities somewhere in the world that are in danger if a nearby volcano erupts or explodes. What would happen to those cities?

The ruins of Pompeii with Mount Vesuvius in background

VOCABULARY PREVIEW

🔊
CD 1, TR 9

A Listen to the following sentences that contain information from the lecture. As you listen, write the word from the box that completes the sentence.

archaeologists	ancient	ash	CE
eruption	metropolitan	ruins	volcanic

1. Many rich people who live in large _____ areas leave the city in the summer and go to the mountains or to the seashore.

2. In the summer of the year 79 _____, a young Roman boy was visiting his uncle at Pompeii.

3. Pliny saw the _____ of the volcano called Mount Vesuvius.

4. Rock and _____ flew through the air.

5. When the eruption was over, Pompeii was buried under 20 feet of _____ rock and ash.

6. In 1748, an Italian farmer digging on his farm uncovered part of a wall of the _____ city of Pompeii.

7. Soon, _____ began to dig in the area.

8. Today, tourists come from all over the world to see the _____ of the famous city of Pompeii.

B Match the words to their definitions.

_____ 1. archeologist

_____ 2. ash

_____ 3. volcanic

_____ 4. ancient

_____ 5. eruption

_____ 6. metropolitan

_____ 7. ruins

_____ 8. CE

a. the time when a volcano explodes and sends hot rock and dust into the air

b. very old or from many years earlier

c. a scientist who studies things left by people who lived long ago

d. the Common Era

e. the remains of destroyed buildings or cities

f. from a volcano

g. a soft, gray powder that is left when something burns

h. of or connected to a large city

PREDICTIONS

Think about the questions in the Topic Preview on page 9 and the sentences you heard in the Vocabulary Preview. Write three questions that you think will be answered in the lecture. Share your questions with your classmates.

NOTETAKING PREPARATION

Using Symbols in Notes

As you learned in Chapter 1, you can use symbols to get information down quickly. Several of these symbols come from mathematics.

<	less than	↑	many, increase, up
>	more than	+	and, also, more than
~	about, approximately	∴	therefore, as a result
→	leads to, then, next, become, go to	#	number
↓	not so many, get less, down	K	thousand

CD 1, TR 10

A Listen to the sentences that contain information from the lecture. As you listen, complete each of the following notes with one of the symbols from the box above.

1. boy look _____ in sky

2. boy _____ fam Rom. historian

3. no time to escape _____ buried alive

4. _____ 2000 ppl died

5. P. forgotten _____ 1700 yrs

Discourse Cues for Chronology

Discourse Cues for Chronology   Listen carefully for words and phrases that tell you when something happened and the order in which something happened. Such words and phrases are particularly important when someone is telling a story.

in [year]	today / one day	for [length of time]
in the winter of [year]	a few years later	as / after / before
[length of time] ago	after [number] years	then / next / later

CD 1, TR 10

B Listen to information from the lecture and write down the chronological discourse cues you hear.

1. _____

2. _____

3. _____

4. _____

5. _____

🔊 FIRST LISTENING
CD 1, TR 11

Listen to the lecture on Pompeii. As you listen, put the following parts of the lecture in the order that you hear them. Number them 1 to 5.

_____ Mount Vesuvius erupted.

_____ Tourists visit the ruins of Pompeii.

_____ Pliny the Younger went to visit Pompeii.

_____ Eighteen thousand people escaped from Pompeii.

_____ Pompeii was completely buried.

🔊 SECOND LISTENING
CD 1, TR 12

Listen to information from the lecture. The speaker will talk slowly and carefully. You don't have to do anything as you listen. Just relax and listen.

THIRD LISTENING

Listen to the lecture in two parts. Follow the directions for each part. When you have finished, review your notes. Later, you will use them to summarize the lecture with a partner.

CD 1, TR 13

Part 1

You will hear the first part of the lecture again. Listen and complete the notes by adding the abbreviations and symbols from the box.

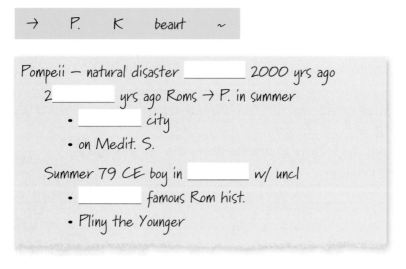

→　　P.　　K　　beaut　　~

Pompeii — natural disaster _____ 2000 yrs ago
　　2_____ yrs ago Roms → P. in summer
　　　• _____ city
　　　• on Medit. S.
　　Summer 79 CE boy in _____ w/ uncl
　　　• _____ famous Rom hist.
　　　• Pliny the Younger

CD 1, TR 13

Part 2

As you listen to the second part of the lecture, take your own notes on a separate piece of paper.

CD 1, TR 14

ACCURACY CHECK

You will hear questions and statements about the lecture. For 1–4, listen to the question and write the letter of the best answer. For 5–8, listen to the statement and write _T_ for _true_ or _F_ for _false_.

_____ 1. a. for holidays
b. in the summer
c. in the fall
d. for vacation

_____ 2. a. 2000 CE
b. 1748 CE
c. 79 CE
d. 1800 CE

_____ 3. a. a volcano
b. a dark cloud
c. a mountain
d. an eruption

_____ 4. a. 79 CE
b. 2,000 years ago
c. 1748
d. 2000 CE

5. _____   6. _____   7. _____   8. _____

ORAL SUMMARY

Use your notes to create an oral summary of the lecture with your partner. As you work together, add details to your notes that your partner included but you had missed.

DISCUSSION

Discuss the following questions with a classmate or in a small group.

1. Why do you think the lecturer explained that Pliny the Younger became a famous historian?

2. If you had lived in Pompeii in 79 CE, what would you have done when the volcano began to erupt?

3. Name some disaster movies that you are familiar with. Why do you think so many people enjoy watching disaster movies?

4. The eruption of Vesuvius was a _natural_ disaster that could not be prevented. But other disasters can be prevented, for example, an explosion at a nuclear power plant. What do you think is the most dangerous situation today that could cause a disaster? What do you think people can do to change the situation?

TASK 1 What Happened First?

CD 1, TR 15

A Listen to two sentences. For each pair of sentences, take notes as your listen.

1.

2.

3.

4.

5.

6.

CD 1, TR 15

B Listen to the two sentences again. Circle *before* if the event in the first sentence happened before the event in the second sentence. Circle *after* if it happened after.

1. The event in Sentence 1 happened **before** / **after** the event in Sentence 2.

2. The event in Sentence 1 happened **before** / **after** the event in Sentence 2.

3. The event in Sentence 1 happened **before** / **after** the event in Sentence 2.

4. The event in Sentence 1 happened **before** / **after** the event in Sentence 2.

5. The event in Sentence 1 happened **before** / **after** the event in Sentence 2.

6. The event in Sentence 1 happened **before** / **after** the event in Sentence 2.

TASK 2 Famous Volcanoes of the World

CD 1, TR 16

A Listen to the short lecture. As you listen, fill in the missing information about the famous volcanoes in the chart below.

Famous Volcanoes of the World			
Name	**Location**	**Date of Eruption**	**Approximate Number of People Who Died**
Vesuvius	Italy	79	2,000
Cotopaxi	Ecuador	1877	
Krakatoa	Indonesia		36,000
Mont Pelée	Martinique	1902	
Mount St. Helens	Washington State (U.S.A.)	1980	
Mount Tambora	Indonesia		

B Check your answers with a partner.

Eruption of Mount Tungurahua in Ecuador

Steve Jobs

A Man with a Vision

TOPIC PREVIEW

Answer the following questions with a partner or your classmates.

1. What electronic tools—a computer, a cell phone, a tablet, etc.—do you use on a daily basis? Which is the one you could not do without? Why?

2. Describe an electronic device you dream of having 25 years from now. Why do you think this type of device would be helpful both to you and others?

3. Who are two people who you think are as famous as Steve Jobs? Explain why.

Steve Jobs

VOCABULARY PREVIEW

CD 1, TR 17

A Listen to the following sentences that contain information from the lecture. As you listen, write the word from the box that completes the sentence.

animated	device	equipment	founded
mass	profitable	released	strategy

1. Jobs' friend Stephen Wozniak liked to design and build his own electronic _____ .

2. Jobs and Wozniak _____ the Apple Computer company.

3. The Apple II became the world's first _____-produced personal computer.

4. The movie *Toy Story* was the first full-length, computer-generated, _____ film.

5. Pixar became a very, very _____ company.

6. In 2001 Jobs introduced Apple's "digital-hub" _____ .

7. The iPhone was like having a computer, a camera, and a phone all in one _____ .

8. Three years later, Jobs _____ the iPad onto the market.

B Match the words to their definitions.

_____ 1. equipment
_____ 2. found
_____ 3. mass
_____ 4. animated
_____ 5. profitable
_____ 6. strategy
_____ 7. device
_____ 8. release

a. in large numbers

b. a method or plan for doing something

c. made by filming many slightly different pictures so they appear to move

d. makes a lot of money for you or your company

e. to start a business

f. to make a product available for sale

g. tools or other items used for a particular purpose

h. a machine used for a special purpose

PREDICTIONS

Think about the questions in the Topic Preview on page 16 and the sentences you heard in the Vocabulary Preview. Write three questions that you think will be answered in the lecture. Share your questions with your classmates.

NOTETAKING PREPARATION

Time Lines

When you are taking notes about a person's life, write the dates and years that you hear underneath one another in the left margin of your notes. Then after the lecture, you can easily turn your notes into a time line that will help you organize the events in that person's life.

1955	Bill Gates b. in Seattle, WA
	prnts want him to be lawyer
1968	→ interested in computers
	wrote 1st prog - tic tac toe game
1973	grad from h.s.; went to Harvard

🔊 CD 1, TR 18

A **Listen to information from the lecture. Circle the letter of the notes that you think create a better time line: *a* or *b*.**

a.

```
1998 → Apple intro iMac
  1 yr later - iBook
2001 → iPod (most pop dig music player)
2007 → iPhone (phone = mini comp)
```

b.

```
1998  Apple intro iMac
1999  iBook
2001  iPod
2007  iPhone = mini comp.
```

B Compare your answer with a partner and explain your choice.

Discourse Cues for Chronology   Remember to listen for words and phrases that tell you when things happened and the order they happened in. Also, when you listen to a history or a biography (the story of someone's life), listen for dates.

🔊 CD 1, TR 18

C **Listen to information from the lecture and write the chronological discourse cues you hear.**

1. _____

2. _____

3. _____

4. _____

5. _____

FIRST LISTENING

CD 1, TR 19

Listen to the lecture about Steve Jobs. As you listen, put the following parts of the lecture in the order that you hear them. Number them 1 to 5.

_____ Jobs returned to Apple.

_____ Jobs introduced the iBook.

_____ Jobs began working with Pixar.

_____ Jobs started Apple Computer with Wozniak.

_____ Jobs introduced the "digital hub" strategy.

SECOND LISTENING

CD 1, TR 20

Listen to information from the lecture. The speaker will talk slowly and carefully. You don't have to do anything as you listen. Just relax and listen.

THIRD LISTENING

Listen to the lecture in two parts. Follow the directions for each part. When you have finished, review your notes. Later, you will use them to summarize the lecture with a partner.

Part 1

CD 1, TR 21

You will hear the first part of the lecture again. Listen and complete the notes by adding the abbreviations and symbols from the box.

| @ | 1st | PC | b. | & |

```
                    Steve Jobs
1955   Jobs _____ in CA — Silicon V.
1969   J. met S. Wozniak — built elec equip
1975   Woz. designed 1st _____
         • J. good _____ bus.
         • J. _____ W. built PCs in gar.
1976   W. & J. started Apple Comp.
1977   Apple → success!
         • _____ mass prod PC
         • Jobs 25 = millionaire
```

Part 2

CD 1, TR 21

As you listen to the second part of the lecture, take your own notes on a separate piece of paper.

ACCURACY CHECK

A You will hear six questions about the lecture. Listen to each question and write the letter of the best answer.

CD 1, TR 22

_____ 1. a. 1955
b. 1956
c. 1975
d. 1976

_____ 4. a. 1955
b. 1975
c. 1985
d. 1995

_____ 2. a. 12
b. 14
c. 16
d. 18

_____ 5. a. 1978
b. 1988
c. 1998
d. 2008

_____ 3. a. 20
b. 21
c. 25
d. 27

_____ 6. a. 1951
b. 1971
c. 1991
d. 2011

B You will hear four questions about the lecture. Write a short answer to each question. Use your notes.

CD 1, TR 22

1. _____

2. _____

3. _____

4. _____

ORAL SUMMARY

Use your notes to create an oral summary of the lecture with your partner. As you work together, add details to your notes that your partner included but you had missed.

DISCUSSION

Discuss the following questions with a classmate or in a small group.

1. What effect do you think the computer and the Internet have had on student life? Name another modern device that has been revolutionary for you.

2. Do you know anyone who might make life in the twenty-first century better or more interesting? Is that person someone you know, or someone you read or heard about?

3. If you were going to spend 10 months alone in a remote area doing research or working on a job, what electronic equipment would you want to have with you? Why?

TASK 1 The Evolution of the Computer

CD 1, TR 23

Listen to a short talk about the evolution of computers. As you listen, add the dates to complete the chart below.

Event in Computer Evolution	Date
The abacus was invented in Babylonia.	
Blaise Pascal invented the first automatic calculator. It did not run on electricity; it ran by turning gears and wheels.	
Gottfried Wilhelm Leibniz designed another type of calculator. It also ran with gears and wheels.	
Joseph-Marie Jacquard invented a weaving loom that used punch cards. This led to the coding used in modern computers.	
Charles Babbage invented all of the parts that are used in the modern computer.	
Herman Hollerith invented a calculating machine that counted and sorted information.	
First-generation computers were very large and used vacuum tubes to run.	
Second-generation computers no longer use vacuum tubes. They run on silicon chips.	
Computers became affordable and small enough to fit in a home.	
Computers start to be much like the computers that are in use today.	

TASK 2 Landmarks in Technology

CD 1, TR 24

A **Listen to descriptions of people and their companies. As you listen, take notes.**

CD 1, TR 24

B **Listen again and answer the questions below. Be ready to do some math to get the right answer!**

1. In what year did Mark Zuckerberg start Facebook? _____

2. In what year did Wikipedia have over 3 million articles? _____

3. In what year did Amazon.com start making profits? _____

4. In what year did Larry Page and Sergey Brin create Google? _____

5. In what year was Bill Gates worth $53 billion? _____

6. In what year was Twitter created? _____

Surviving an Avalanche

TOPIC PREVIEW

Look at the photo of an avalanche on this page. Then answer the following questions with a partner.

1. Where do avalanches happen? What causes them?

2. What do you think someone might be doing to get caught in an avalanche?

3. How likely is it for someone to survive an avalanche?

VOCABULARY PREVIEW

A **Read the definitions of these key words and phrases that you will hear during the video.**

snap break suddenly with a short, sharp noise

crushed pressed so hard that something is made flat or broken into pieces

resurfaced came back up to the top

eventually in the end, especially after a long time

unbearable too bad or painful to continue experiencing

hundreds of tons an extreme amount of weight (1 ton = 2,240 lbs or 1,016 kg)

magnitude the size or importance of something

pause stop for a short time

popped right out came out suddenly and forcefully from a small space

B Work with a partner and write in the blank the word or phrase from the box that best completes the sentence.

bottom	flying down	for a moment	fortunately
half	power	showed up	weight

1. As the skier felt the _____ of the avalanche, he **paused** _____ to appreciate the **magnitude** of the event. **Hundreds of tons** of snow were _____ the mountain.

2. The avalanche caused the trees to **snap** in _____.

3. The skier thought he would be **crushed** by the **unbearable** _____ of the snow, but _____ he **popped right out** of the snow.

4. He reached the _____ of the mountain and **resurfaced**, and **eventually** his friends _____.

VIEWING

🖥 FIRST VIEWING

Watch the video, and then compare your first impressions with a partner. Talk about what you remember, what surprised you, and what interested you.

🖥 SECOND VIEWING

Watch the video again. Listen for the missing words and write them in the blanks.

1. The temperatures were _____ pretty significantly so there was a lot of _____ happening in the snow pack.

2. For a moment, actually, I stopped being _____.

3. You don't _____ feel that kind of power ever, especially in an uncontrolled environment.

4. I looked down and I could see the entire avalanche _____, and it was all—I knew I was going to the bottom of the _____.

5. I got to the bottom. I could feel it _____ down, and I popped right out at the toe of the avalanche.

LAWINENGEFAHR
DANGER D' AVALANCHES
DANGER OF AVALANCHES

🖵 THIRD VIEWING

Complete these notes as you watch the video. Use abbreviations and symbols as necessary.

```
1) 2 mths ago _____
   • went _____ ft
   • at time was _____ w/_____
2) Watched mtn crack
   • watched trees _____
   • _____ for a while
   • eventually _____
   • thnking never _____
   • for a mo, stop'd _____
3) Back into snow pack
   • _____
   • _____
   • _____
4) 20 mins _____
   • 100% sure _____
   • couldn't _____
```

ORAL SUMMARY

Use your notes to create an oral summary of the video with your partner. As you work together, add details to your notes that your partner included but you had missed.

DISCUSSION

Discuss the following questions with a classmate or in a small group.

1. Jimmy Chin says, "They would have been less surprised if they had been talking to my ghost." What does he mean by this?

2. How do you think Jimmy Chin felt before, during, immediately after, and a few weeks after the avalanche?

3. Jimmy Chin was in what was probably the most frightening situation of his life. What was the scariest situation you have ever experienced? Tell the story.

Process

Describing How Things Work

Containers moving through the
Port of Singapore Authority

Roller Coasters

The Ups and Downs of How They Work

TOPIC PREVIEW

Answer the following questions with a partner or your classmates.

1. Have you ever been to an amusement park? If you went to an amusement park today, what kind of ride would you go on? What ride do you think would be the most fun?

2. What kinds of activities do you think little children, young adults, and old people enjoy doing for a day of fun?

3. Why do you think people will pay money to take a roller-coaster ride or do something else that scares them? Give at least two reasons.

Riding a roller coaster
at an amusement park
in Essen, Germany

VOCABULARY PREVIEW

CD 2, TR 1

A Listen to the following sentences that contain information from the lecture. As you listen, write the word or phrase from the box that completes the sentence.

consists of	coming off	gain	gravity	loop
path	physics	sets	slope	

1. Let's talk about the _____ involved in a ride on a roller coaster.

2. A simple roller coaster _____ a frame with a track on it.

3. The track follows a _____ that ends at the same place it started.

4. The roller-coaster cars have two _____ of wheels.

5. The wheels below the track keep the fast-moving cars from _____ the track.

6. At the top of the first hill, the chain comes off the cars and _____ takes over.

7. The cars _____ speed as they roll downhill.

8. Then they go down a very steep _____.

9. The cars travel in a _____ that puts us upside down.

B Match the words to their definitions.

_____ 1. loop
_____ 2. come off
_____ 3. slope
_____ 4. gravity
_____ 5. consist of
_____ 6. set
_____ 7. physics
_____ 8. gain
_____ 9. path

a. the force that causes objects to fall to the ground

b. the side of a hill, or a surface that is higher at one end

c. to stop being on or attached to something else

d. to increase in amount

e. to be made up of something

f. a circle made when something curves around and crosses itself

g. a group of things that are similar and are used together

h. the direction or route that something follows

i. the study of energy and matter

PREDICTIONS

Think about the questions in the Topic Preview on page 26 and the sentences you heard in the Vocabulary Preview. Write three questions that you think will be answered in the lecture. Share your questions with your classmates.

NOTETAKING PREPARATION

Steps in a Process

When a speaker describes a process, use numbers in your notes to identify the different steps in the process. Write the name of the process above the numbered steps. Indent the numbered steps.

How ~~~~~~~ ~~~ ~~~~~ ~~
  1. ~~~ ~~ ~~~~ ~~
  2. ~~ ~~~ ~ ~~~~
  3. ~~~~ ~~~
  4. ~~ ~~~~~ ~~~~

CD 2, TR 2

A **Listen to a brief summary of information from the lecture. Circle the letter of the notes below that best record what you hear.**

a.

How roller coasters work
  1. Chain pulls cars ↑ hill
  2. Chain off – g. push ↓ hill v. fast
  3. Bottom – e. to go ↑ next hill

b.

How roller coasters work
  1. Cars go ↑ hill
  2. Grav push cars
  3. Cars go downhill v. fast ↓
  4. Now have eng – go up next hill

B **Work with a partner and discuss your choice and why you made it.**

Discourse Cues for a Process

When a speaker is describing a process, listen for words and phrases such as the following that signal the steps in the process.

first	then	the first thing that happens is
second	next	during this stage
third	finally	at this point

CD 2, TR 2

C **Listen to information from the lecture and write the process discourse cues you hear.**

1. _____

2. _____

3. _____

4. _____

FIRST LISTENING

CD 2, TR 3

Listen to the lecture on how roller coasters work. As you listen, put the following parts of the lecture in the order that you hear them. Number them 1 to 5.

_____ Start of roller-coaster ride

_____ Summary of the roller-coaster process

_____ The speaker's attitude toward roller coasters

_____ The role of gravity in pushing roller-coaster cars around the track

_____ Description of a simple roller coaster

SECOND LISTENING

CD 2, TR 4

Listen to information from the lecture. The speaker will talk slowly and carefully. You don't have to do anything as you listen. Just relax and listen.

THIRD LISTENING

Listen to the lecture in two parts. Follow the directions for each part. When you have finished, review your notes. Later, you will use them to summarize the lecture with a partner.

Part 1

CD 2, TR 5

You will hear the first part of the lecture again. Listen and complete the notes by adding the abbreviations and symbols from the box.

whls	RCs	=	v.	w/

Topic = How roller coasters work — physics of _____
- simple RC = frame _____ track, like train
- track _____ hill + curves
- cars — _____ fast
- cars — 2 sets whls
- _____ below — keep cars on

Part 2

CD 2, TR 5

As you listen to the second part of the lecture, take your own notes on a separate piece of paper.

ACCURACY CHECK

CD 2, TR 6

A You will hear six questions about the lecture. Listen to each question and write the letter of the best answer.

_____ 1. a. a frame with a track on it
b. a structure with wheels on it
c. a path for workers to walk on
d. a loop to send the cars around

_____ 2. a. a bicycle
b. a car
c. a train
d. a wagon

_____ 3. a. gravity
b. energy
c. speed
d. chain

_____ 4. a. the track
b. the cars
c. gravity
d. speed

_____ 5. a. biology
b. physics
c. chemistry
d. astronomy

_____ 6. a. Chains stop the cars.
b. Hills become less steep.
c. Cars gain energy.
d. The ride is frightening.

CD 2, TR 6

B You will hear five questions about the lecture. Write a short answer to each question. Use your notes.

1. _____

2. _____

3. _____

4. _____

5. _____

ORAL SUMMARY

Use your notes to create an oral summary of the lecture with your partner. As you work together, add details to your notes that your partner included but you had missed.

DISCUSSION

Discuss the following questions with a classmate or in a small group.

1. Look at the picture on page 26 of people on an amusement park ride. What kind of a ride do you think they are on? Would you go for ride on it? Why or why not?

2. Compare the amusement park ride in the picture on page 26 with the one on this page. What do you think are the differences between them? Which one do you think would be the most thrilling, dangerous, and fun?

3. What role do you think gravity and energy play in the ride in the picture on this page?

TASK 1 Taking a Pulse

CD 2, TR 7

A Listen to someone describe how to take a pulse. As you listen, fill in the missing words in the sentences below.

Taking your pulse is easy. Just follow these _____.
1

First, have a watch with a _____ hand ready or use the
2
stopwatch on your cell phone.

To start with, put the middle three _____ of your
3
right hand on your left wrist just
below your thumb. Press down
a little until you

_____ your pulse
4
beat. Can you feel your pulse?

Look at the second hand on your watch and start _____ the beats that
5
you are feeling with your fingers. _____ 30 seconds, stop counting and
6
write down the _____ of beats that you felt in 30 seconds.
7

Wait a few seconds and then repeat the _____. Write down the
8
second number and _____ it to the first number. This is your
9
pulse _____.
10

B Have a classmate read the above steps while you take your pulse.

TASK 2 Yoga Poses

(A) Make sure that you know the meaning of the following words. Work with a partner and point to these parts of the body.

chin   back   toes   bottom   stomach   knees   forehead

CD 2, TR 8

(B) Listen to someone describe how to do six different yoga poses. As you listen, match the pictures below with the pose that is described. Write the number of the pose in the box on the picture.

CD 2, TR 8

(C) Listen again and follow the steps to do one of the yoga poses.

Language

How Children Acquire Theirs

TOPIC PREVIEW

Answer the following questions with a partner or your classmates.

1. How do parents and other adults communicate with new babies? And how do new babies let adults know what they want or need?

2. Does a month-old baby who hears only Korean make the same sounds as one who hears English or Russian? Or do these different babies make different languagelike sounds?

3. When do children begin to say words? How do they learn vocabulary and grammar? Do they make mistakes?

A student in Orissa, India

VOCABULARY PREVIEW

CD 2, TR 9

A Listen to the following sentences that contain information from the lecture. As you listen, write the word from the box that completes the sentence.

acquire	babble	backgrounds	cooing
environment	essential	invent	overgeneralize

1. A few weeks after birth, babies start to make _____ noises when they're happy.

2. Around four months of age, babies begin to _____.

3. By 10 months old, the babbling of babies from different language _____ sounds different.

4. At first, babies _____ their own words for things.

5. In the next few months, babies will _____ a lot of words.

6. These words are usually the names of things that are in the baby's

   _____.

7. The speech young children produce is often called "telegraphic" speech because they leave out all but the most _____ words.

8. Babies begin to _____ a grammar rule and make a lot of grammar mistakes.

B Match the words to their definitions.

_____ 1. environment   a. to make something new

_____ 2. essential   b. your family, community, and other things that affect you

_____ 3. acquire   c. the place you usually are and the things in it

_____ 4. coo   d. to gain or learn something

_____ 5. invent   e. to make soft, gentle sounds

_____ 6. background   f. necessary or most important

_____ 7. babble   g. to apply something, such as a rule, at all times

_____ 8. overgeneralize   h. to make speechlike sounds

PREDICTIONS

Think about the questions in the Topic Preview on page 33 and the sentences you heard in the Vocabulary Preview. Write three questions that you think will be answered in the lecture. Share your questions with your classmates.

NOTETAKING PREPARATION

Abbreviating Frequently Repeated Words

When you are listening to a lecture, you will often hear the same words repeated several times. Create special abbreviations for these words in the following ways.

- For the most important word in the lecture, use only the first letter of the word. Make it a capital letter and put a period after it.

    L. = language

- Take out all the vowels in the word.

    bb / bbs = baby / babies

- Use the first few letters of the word.

    ch = children; *comm* = communication

A Make abbreviations for the following frequently repeated words in the lecture.

1. words _____

2. past tense _____

3. verbs _____

4. acquire / acquisition _____

5. babble / babbling _____

6. first language _____

CD 2, TR 10

B Listen to sentences from the lecture and fill in the blanks with abbreviations you created in **A.**

1. All bbs in world begin _____ ~ same age

2. Next stage of L. _____ begin ~ 18 mths

3. In next mths bbs _____ a lot _____

4. E.g., begin learn rules _____ of _____

5. Think → how is _____ and 2nd _____ diff/sim

Discourse Cues for a Process Listen for cues that show that a lecturer is going to describe a process. Listen for phrases such as

This is how . . .   *How to . . .*   *The way that . . .*

CD 2, TR 10

C Listen to the opening of the lecture and circle the best title for the process that the speaker is going to describe.

a. How Chldrn Develop

b. How BBs Comm

c. How Chldrn Learn 1st L.

d. How Studs Learn 2nd L.

FIRST LISTENING

CD 2, TR 11

Listen to the lecture on child language development. As you listen, put the following parts of the lecture in the order that you hear them. Number them 1 to 5.

_____ Children make past-tense verb mistakes.

_____ Babies make babbling noises.

_____ Babies use telegraphic speech.

_____ Students are asked to think about first and second language learning processes.

_____ Babies make one-word sentences.

SECOND LISTENING

CD 2, TR 12

Listen to information from the lecture. The speaker will talk slowly and carefully. You don't have to do anything as you listen. Just relax and listen.

THIRD LISTENING

Listen to the lecture in two parts. Follow the directions for each part. When you have finished, review your notes. Later, you will use them to summarize the lecture with a partner.

Part 1

CD 2, TR 13

You will hear the first part of the lecture again. Listen and complete the notes by adding the abbreviations and symbols from the box.

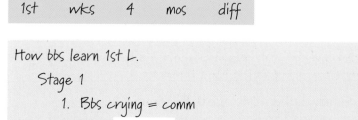

| 1st | wks | 4 | mos | diff |

How bbs learn 1st L.
    Stage 1
        1. Bbs crying = comm
        2. Few _____ old = cooing
        3. _____ mos = start bbl
        4. 10 _____ = bbl _____ for diff Ls
    Stage 2
        1. _____ wds

Part 2

CD 2, TR 13

As you listen to the second part of the lecture, take your own notes on a separate piece of paper.

ACCURACY CHECK

CD 2, TR 14

You will hear questions and statements about the lecture. For 1–3, listen to the question and write the letter of the best answer. For 4–7, listen to the statement and write *T* for *true* or *F* for *false*.

_____ 1. a. birth
        b. 4 months
        c. 10 months
        d. 18 months

_____ 2. a. kiki
        b. Daddy, up.
        c. I walked home.
        d. I goed to bed.

_____ 3. a. 10 to 12 months
        b. 8 to 24 months
        c. 2 to 3 years
        d. 7 to 8 years

4. _____   5. _____   6. _____   7. _____

ORAL SUMMARY

Use your notes to create an oral summary of the lecture with your partner. As you work together, add details to your notes that your partner included but you had missed.

DISCUSSION

Discuss the following statements with a classmate or in a small group.

1. Parents understand what their baby needs even before the baby begins to talk.

2. It's easy for a baby to learn his or her language, but it's hard work for an adult to learn a second or foreign language.

3. Everyone should learn to speak the dominant language of the country where they live even if a different language is spoken in their home.

4. It would be better if everybody in the world spoke the same language.

TASK 1 Stages in Language Development

🔊 CD 2, TR 15

A Listen to these English-speaking babies and children. Write down what you hear each one say.

1. _____

2. _____

3. _____

4. _____

5. _____

B Compare your answers in **A** with a partner. Discuss the meaning of what each baby said.

🔊 CD 2, TR 15

C Listen again. Draw a line to match the speech of each child, 1 to 5, to a stage of language development that you learned about in the lecture. The first one is done for you.

1 Babbling

2 One-word speech

3 Telegraphic speech

4 Overgeneralize past tense

5 Multiword speech

TASK 2 Writing an E-mail

🔊 CD 2, TR 16

A Listen and write down the five tips, or steps, in writing effective e-mail messages. You will hear each tip twice.

1. _____

2. _____

3. _____

4. _____

5. _____

B Check your answers with a partner. Then, with your partner, decide on one or two more rules that you think would be helpful.

CHAPTER 6

Robots

How They Work and Learn to Work

TOPIC PREVIEW

Answer the following questions with a partner or your classmates.

1. What do you picture when you think of "a robot"? What does it look like? What does it do? Draw a simple picture of your robot.

2. Have you seen a movie or TV show in which robots play an important role? What was the name of the movie? What did the robots do in the movie? How do "real" robots differ from "movie" robots?

3. What will robots look like and be doing in 10 years? in 20 years? in 50 years?

A student builds a robot.

VOCABULARY PREVIEW

CD 3, TR 1

A Listen to the following sentences that contain information from the lecture. As you listen, write the word from the box that completes the sentence.

assembly	autonomous	detect	efficiently	guidance
industrial	precise	repetitive	sensors	stores

1. Today, I'm going to talk mostly about _____ robots.

2. These robots do work that is _____, dangerous, or boring.

3. The robot learns to do its job with the _____ of a human being.

4. Robotic arms on the _____ line join the parts of a car together.

5. Robots are very _____ when repeating a task.

6. Robots do work humans could do, but they do it more _____.

7. The robot _____ the exact movements in its computer memory.

8. A robot uses _____ to gather information.

9. An _____ machine can change its behavior in relation to its surroundings.

10. Honda's ASIMO can _____ the movements of people nearby.

B Match the words to their definitions.

_____ 1. detect   a. over and over in the same way each time

_____ 2. precise   b. used in industry and manufacturing

_____ 3. autonomous   c. a device that reacts to change in light, heat, sound, etc.

_____ 4. industrial   d. to save information to be used again

_____ 5. store   e. to find or become aware of something

_____ 6. repetitive   f. help, assistance, and direction

_____ 7. guidance   g. the process of putting something together

_____ 8. assembly   h. done quickly and correctly

_____ 9. sensor   i. accurate and correct

_____ 10. efficiently   j. independent; able to act alone

PREDICTIONS

Think about the questions in the Topic Preview on page 39 and the sentences you heard in the Vocabulary Preview. Write three questions that you think will be answered in the lecture. Share your questions with your classmates.

NOTETAKING PREPARATION

Listening for New Sections of a Lecture

Different sections of a lecture deal with different aspects of the lecturer's chosen topic. As you listen to a lecture, listen for when the lecturer moves from one aspect of the topic to a new aspect. When that happens, leave a space and start a new section in your notes.

A section of a lecture may, for example, give a definition, provide historical background, analyze reasons, or describe a process.

A lecturer will use language such as the following to introduce a new section:

I'd like to start by defining . . .
Now, let's talk about why . . .
So what is the process by which . . .
Next, I want to examine the history of . . .

🔊 CD 3, TR 2

A Listen to three section openings from the lecture. Take notes.

1.

2.

3.

🔊 CD 3, TR 2

B Listen again to the section openings from the lecture. Circle what you think the lecturer will go on to talk about in each section.

1. a. historical background   b. a process   c. a description   d. a definition

2. a. historical background   b. a process   c. a description   d. a definition

3. a. historical background   b. a process   c. a description   d. a definition

Discourse Cues for a Process   When you listen to steps in a process, remember to listen for language that signals the different steps. Review the discourses cues on pages 28 and 35.

🔊 CD 3, TR 2

C Listen to sentences from the lecture. Write the cue you hear in each sentence that shows the lecturer is describing a step in a process.

1. _____   4. _____

2. _____   5. _____

3. _____

FIRST LISTENING

CD 3, TR 3

Listen to the lecture on robots. As you listen, put the following parts of the lecture in the order that you hear them. Number them 1 to 5.

_____ How robots learn their job

_____ Robots more effective than humans

_____ An example of an autonomous machine

_____ Automatic robots

_____ Robots on factory assembly lines

SECOND LISTENING

CD 3, TR 4

Listen to information from the lecture. The speaker will talk slowly and carefully. You don't have to do anything as you listen. Just relax and listen.

THIRD LISTENING

Listen to the lecture in two parts. Follow the directions for each part. When you have finished, review your notes. Later, you will use them to summarize the lecture with a partner.

CD 3, TR 5

Part 1

You will hear the first part of the lecture again. Listen and complete the notes by adding the abbreviations and symbols from the box.

machs	e.g.	contr	Rs	=

1) what robots lk like
   - not humans
   - _____
2) today's topic _____ Indust Rs
   - Rs do wk — rep, dang, boring
   - most _____ wk in factories, _____ ptg lids on jars
   - in car facts Rs — very precise
   - Rs do human wk more effic'ly and precisely
3) how rbts wk
   - rbts 1st need _____ syst

CD 3, TR 5

Part 2

As you listen to the second part of the lecture, take your own notes on a separate piece of paper.

ACCURACY CHECK

🔊 CD 3, TR 6

A You will hear six questions about the lecture. Listen to each question and write the letter of the best answer.

_____ 1. a. easy
b. human
c. repetitive
d. interesting

_____ 2. a. jars of fruit
b. parts of cars
c. wheels on tires
d. bolts on wheels

_____ 3. a. sensor
b. power
c. control system
d. arms and legs

_____ 4. a. an automatic robot
b. an industrial machine
c. a handheld computer
d. its brain

_____ 5. a. with the guidance of a human being
b. with the help of another robot
c. with its arms and hands
d. with its moving parts

_____ 6. a. find it
b. lift and move it
c. determine its weight
d. determine the amount of force to use

🔊 CD 3, TR 6

B You will hear four questions about the lecture. Write a short answer to each question. Use your notes.

1. _____

2. _____

3. _____

4. _____

ORAL SUMMARY

Use your notes to create an oral summary of the lecture with your partner. As you work together, add details to your notes that your partner included but you had missed.

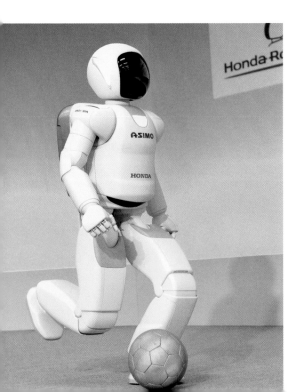

Honda R...

DISCUSSION

Discuss the following questions with a classmate or in a small group.

1. Robots do many jobs in factories that people used to do. What are some of the reasons why robots are now used for these jobs? Do robots put people out of work?

2. Robots will continue to become more humanlike until they look, talk, and think much like human beings. Is this a good thing or a bad thing? Why?

3. 3-D printers already exist. In the future similar machines could use nanobots—robots too small to see—to turn raw materials into new products. Is this a good idea? Why?

TASK 1 Steps in Doing Research

CD 3, TR 7

A **Listen to someone describe the steps in doing research. As you listen, match the steps below to the pictures. Write the number of the step next to the picture.**

Step 1: Do background research.

Step 2: Conduct your experiment.

Step 3: Make observations.

Step 4: Record and analyze your results.

Step 5: Present your research.

Step _____

Step _____

Step _____

Step _____

Step _____

B **Compare your answers with a partner and explain your choices.**

TASK 2 A Simple Experiment

CD 3, TR 8 **A** Listen to things you will need to perform a simple experiment. Write each one next to its picture.

_____

_____

_____

_____

_____

CD 3, TR 8 **B** Listen to the description of the experiment. As you listen, fill in the missing words in the sentences below.

First, pour some _____ into the bottle until it is about one-_____ full. Next, use the _____ to pour some baking soda
1   3
into the _____. After _____, carefully stretch the balloon
4   5
over the _____ of the bottle. Make sure you don't _____ any
6   7
baking _____ into the bottle! Next, _____ up the heavy part
8   9
of the balloon so that the baking soda _____ into the bottle.
10

C Work with a partner. Talk about what you think will happen next.

CD 3, TR 8 **D** Listen to the description of the end of the experiment. Was your guess correct?

Tristan da Cunha Oil Spill

TOPIC PREVIEW

Work with a partner and describe the picture on this page. Discuss how this happened and what steps people will take now to help the birds and their environment. Write the steps below.

VOCABULARY PREVIEW

A Read the definitions of these key words and phrases that you will hear during the video.

remotest farthest away from places where people live

inhabited having people living in or on it

devastating causing a lot of damage or destruction

endangered likely to be harmed or damaged, and possibly die and disappear

transmit images send photos or videos

off the grid not connected to public energy or communication networks

got picked up was reported on by a newspaper or a news program

got it out made sure people heard about it

capturing recording events, usually with photographs or video

B Work with a partner and write vocabulary from **A** in the blanks in the sentences.

1. Tristan da Cunha, one of the _____ islands in the world, is _____ by fewer than 300 people.

2. The island is outside the area of a satellite signal and, therefore, _____.

3. _____ a news event on camera when it happens is the goal of every news photographer.

4. They were able to _____ of the _____ destruction even though they were in the middle of the Pacific Ocean.

5. The birds on the island were an _____ species.

6. Andrew Evans' story _____ by the news media very quickly, but it was *National Geographic* that first _____ to the public.

🖵 FIRST VIEWING

Watch the video, and then compare your first impressions with a partner. Talk about what you remember, what surprised you, and what interested you.

🖵 SECOND VIEWING

Watch the video again. Listen for the missing words and write them in the blanks.

1. It was a big _____ spill that affected a lot of Northern Rock Hopper Penguins.

2. This is an _____ that's completely disconnected. It's off the grid.

3. But _____ are important because they're organic.

4. They published it. They got it _____ there in the real press.

5. This is something that _____ of you can do and _____ of you are doing all the time.

A boat sinks off the coast of Tristan da Cunha, spilling oil.

Complete these notes as you watch the video. Write only important words, not full sentences, and abbreviate common words.

1) Arr. T. da C. — saw _____
   • devastating
   • affect. pengs — _____
2) Alone there — no comm w/_____
3) Steps A.E. took
   1. took pics
   2. _____ vid.
   3. pub it
   4. + _____
   5. Tweeted it
   6. put on _____
   7. N.G. _____
   8. N.Y.T. _____
4) All of you can
   _____
   _____

ORAL SUMMARY

Use your notes to create an oral summary of the video with your partner. As you work together, add details to your notes that your partner included but you had missed.

DISCUSSION

Discuss the following questions with a classmate or in a small group.

1. In the video, you see a newspaper headline "You Really Shouldn't Crash Your Oil Tanker Where a National Geographic Photographer Is." Explain this headline.

2. Andrew Evans suggests that today with our cell phones and the Internet, we can all be reporters. What are some dangers of the general public spreading news this way?

3. Have you ever witnessed a newsworthy event while it happened? Did you or anyone you were with communicate it to others in any way to "get the news out"?

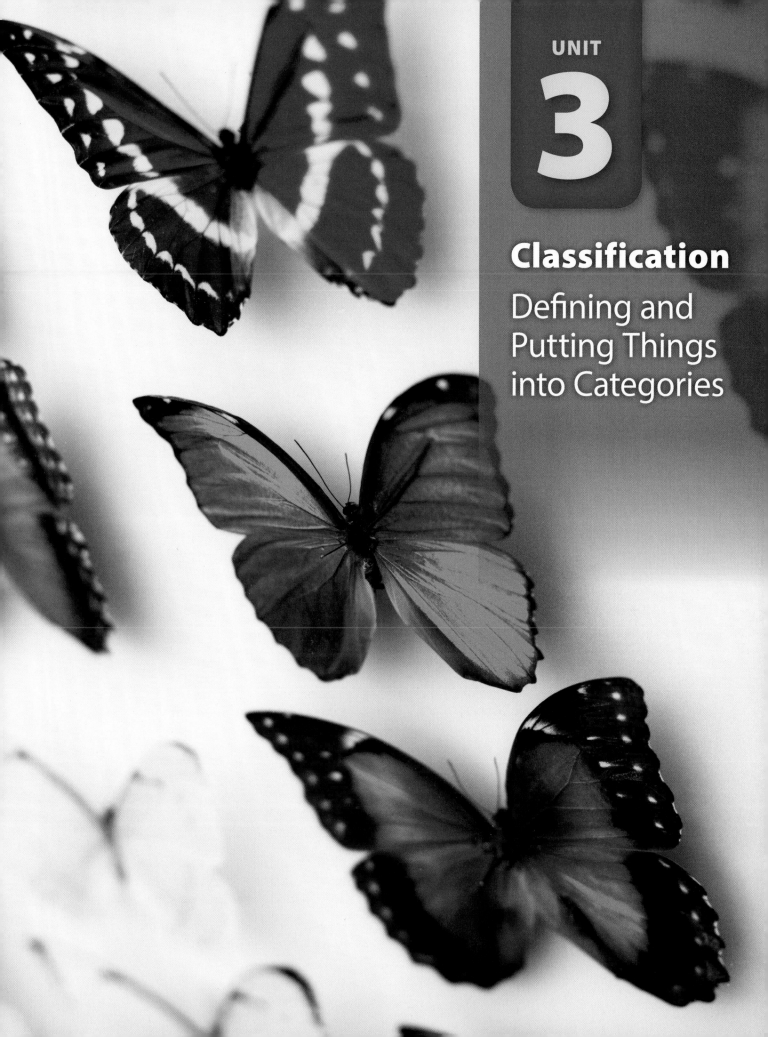

Classification

Defining and
Putting Things
into Categories

A Tidal Wave

What Is It? Can We Predict It?

TOPIC PREVIEW

Answer the following questions with a partner or your classmates.

1. Have you ever experienced an earthquake, a volcano, or a terrible storm? Describe the experience. What happened? What did you do? How did you survive?

2. What is the difference between a tidal wave and a normal ocean wave? What causes each one?

3. Where and when have there been large earthquakes and tidal waves in recent years? What happened? How destructive were they?

A tsunami pours into the city of Miyako, Japan, March 11, 2011.

VOCABULARY PREVIEW

CD 3, TR 9

A Listen to the following sentences that contain information from the lecture. As you listen, write the word from the box that completes the sentence.

crisis	destructive	massive	merging	predict
rushing	shifts	storms	trembles	warn

1. A tidal wave is a very large and _____ wall of water.

2. A tidal wave comes _____ in suddenly and unexpectedly at any time.

3. Do you know that tidal waves are not caused by _____?

4. When an earthquake takes place under the ocean, the ocean floor shakes and

   _____.

5. Sometimes the ocean floor _____ during an underwater earthquake.

6. A double-wave tsunami can also be called a _____ tsunami.

7. In 2011, a _____ earthquake occurred off the coast of Japan.

8. A tsunami caused a _____ at a nuclear plant in northeastern Japan.

9. Today scientists can _____ that a tidal wave will hit land.

10. It is possible to _____ people that a tidal wave is coming.

B Match the words to their definitions.

_____ 1. crisis   a. to mix two or more things together into one

_____ 2. destructive   b. to change position

_____ 3. merge   c. a very difficult or dangerous situation

_____ 4. predict   d. to tell someone of a possible problem or danger

_____ 5. rush   e. causing or able to cause serious damage

_____ 6. shift   f. to say that a particular thing will happen

_____ 7. massive   g. bad weather with a lot of wind
and rain or snow

_____ 8. storm

_____ 9. tremble   h. to shake from side to side

                           i. extremely large

_____ 10. warn   j. to move very quickly

PREDICTIONS

Think about the questions in the Topic Preview on page 50 and the sentences you heard in the Vocabulary Preview. Write three questions that you think will be answered in the lecture. Share your questions with your classmates.

NOTETAKING PREPARATION

Recording Definitions

In a talk, it is sometimes necessary for the speaker to define some of the terms used in the lecture. Usually the lecturer will give a *positive* definition, that is, the speaker will tell you what something is or what it means. Sometimes, however, a speaker may give a *negative* definition and tell you what something is not or what it does *not* mean.

When taking notes, the following symbols are useful abbreviations for showing positive and negative definitions:

Positive definition   =
Negative definition   ≠

A tidal wave is a destructive wall of water   TW = destr wall H$_2$O

CD 3, TR 10

A Listen to the following positive and negative definitions of terms used in the lecture. Use either the symbol = or ≠ to complete the notes below.

1. TW _____ a wave ← tide

2. tsunami _____ TW

3. double tsunami _____ 2 TWs together

4. v. big waves at sea _____ TWs

Discourse Cues for Definition and Classification   Listen for words and phrases that tell you the lecturer is giving you a definition. These are some cues that the lecturer may use to define a term:

is/are (known as) . . .   *can be defined as* . . .
is a type of . . .   *means* . . .

CD 3, TR 10

B Listen to the definitions of some terms in the lecture. As you listen, write the word or phrase from the box that completes the definition.

means	can be defined as	is a type of	is

1. A tidal wave _____ a very large and destructive wave.

2. To quake _____ to move up and down very quickly or to shake.

3. A true tide _____ the normal rise and fall of ocean water at regular times each day.

4. A seismograph _____ instrument for measuring earthquakes.

FIRST LISTENING

Listen to the lecture on tidal waves. As you listen, put the following parts of the lecture in the order that you hear them. Number them 1 to 5.

_____ Predicting earthquakes

_____ The tsunami of March 2011

_____ An overview of the lecture

_____ Definition of a tidal wave

_____ Cause of tidal waves

SECOND LISTENING

Listen to information from the lecture. The speaker will talk slowly and carefully. You don't have to do anything as you listen. Just relax and listen.

THIRD LISTENING

Listen to the lecture in two parts. Follow the directions for each part. When you have finished, review your notes. Later, you will use them to summarize the lecture with a partner.

Part 1

You will hear the first part of the lecture again. Listen and complete the notes by adding the abbreviations and symbols from the box.

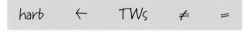

harb	←	TWs	≠	=

> Tidal Waves
> 1. What is a TW?
>   - _____ = destr wall of H₂O
>   - rushes into land
>   - scients call tsunamis
>   - tsun = Jap word _____ harbor wave
>   - wave = tallest in _____, nr land
> 2. TWs _____ normal waves
>   - norm wave ← tides
>   - TW _____ EQs under water

Part 2

As you listen to the second part of the lecture, take your own notes on a separate piece of paper.

CD 3, TR 14

ACCURACY CHECK

You will hear eight questions about the lecture. Listen to each question and choose the correct answer from the box and write it on the line.

double-wave tsunami	harbor	harbor wave	ocean floor
seismograph	tidal wave	tide	wall of water

1. _____

2. _____

3. _____

4. _____

5. _____

6. _____

7. _____

8. _____

ORAL SUMMARY

Use your notes to create an oral summary of the lecture with your partner. As you work together, add details to your notes that your partner included but you had missed.

DISCUSSION

Discuss the following questions with a classmate or in a small group.

1. What is the worst kind of natural disaster: an earthquake, a hurricane, a wildfire, a tidal wave, a volcano eruption, or something else? Explain the reason for your choice.

2. Which of the following natural disasters is easiest to predict: an earthquake, a hurricane, a tornado, a tidal wave, a volcano eruption? Explain the reason for your choice.

3. Do you know what to do if there is an earthquake, a hurricane, a flood, or a tornado? What do you think you should do if one of them happened?

TASK 1 Listening for Definitions

CD 3, TR 15

A Listen to the clues and write the words in the spaces in the crossword puzzle. The clues are definitions. The first answer, 1 across, will be given to you.

CD 3, TR 15

B Listen to the crossword puzzle answers. Check your answers and fill in any that you missed.

TASK 2 Natural Disasters

CD 3, TR 16

Listen to a description of four natural disasters and fill in the missing information in the chart.

Category of Disaster by Cause	Event	Location	Date of Event	Approximate Number of Casualties
Geological	landslide		1958	
Meteorological		Bangladesh		1,300 people
Hydrological			1887	
Space	asteroid explosion			

8

Levels of Language

Formal and Informal

TOPIC PREVIEW

Answer the following questions with a partner or your classmates.

1. Have you ever said something in English, and the person you were speaking with looked at you with surprise or confusion? What kind of mistake did you make?

2. When you meet your friend's mother, is it more correct to say, "Hi, Jennifer" or "Hello, Mrs. Collier"? Why do you think your choice is the right one?

3. If you were talking to a friend about a teacher you like, would you be more likely to say, "Jones is a great teacher" or "Doctor Jones is a truly great educator"? Explain your choice.

Friends chat as sand blows around them in the Libyan desert.

VOCABULARY PREVIEW

CD 4, TR 1

A **Listen to the following sentences that contain information from the lecture. As you listen, write the word from the box that completes the sentence.**

authority	ceremonies	colleagues	interacting
polite	reference	tend	usage

1. Today I want to talk about levels of language _____.

2. Formal written language is the kind you find in _____ books such as encyclopedias.

3. People usually use formal English at _____ such as graduations.

4. We also _____ to use formal language in conversations with persons we don't know well.

5. Formal language tends to be more _____.

6. Informal language is used in conversation with _____, family, and friends.

7. I might say to a friend, "Close the door, please." To someone in _____ I would say, "Excuse me, could you please close the door?"

8. The difference between formal and informal usage can be learned by observing and _____ with native speakers.

B **Match the words to their definitions.**

_____ 1. ceremony   a. containing facts and other information

_____ 2. colleague   b. to usually happen or to be likely to happen

_____ 3. authority   c. to talk to other people when doing something together

_____ 4. interact

_____ 5. usage   d. a formal event on a special occasion

_____ 6. reference   e. behaving in a way that shows respect for others

_____ 7. tend   f. the power or responsibility to make decisions

_____ 8. polite   g. a person you work with

                  h. the way words are used

PREDICTIONS

Think about the questions in the Topic Preview on page 56 and the sentences you heard in the Vocabulary Preview. Write three questions that you think will be answered in the lecture. Share your questions with your classmates.

NOTETAKING PREPARATION

Listening for Examples

A good lecturer will always make concepts clearer by providing good examples. Listen for language that tells you that the lecturer is going to introduce an example, such as the following:

For example	*Let me illustrate*
For instance	*Such as*
Let me give you an example	

When you hear an example, write the example below the concept that is being defined and indent your notes. Many notetakers introduce the example with one of these abbreviations:

e.g.
ex.

A **Listen to a part of the lecture while you look at the notes below. After you listen, rewrite the notes in a clearer notetaking format.**

CD 4, TR 2

Diff betwn form & inform vocab
When talkng to friend
ex. — use crazy about
w/boss use really enjoy

Discourse Cues for Definition and Classification
Listen for cues that show the lecturer is going to give an example. Make sure you include the example in your notes. This will help you understand the lecture.

B **Listen to five sentences that contain information from the lecture. As you listen, write the language cue in each sentence that the lecturer uses to introduce an example.**

CD 4, TR 2

1. _____

2. _____

3. _____

4. _____

5. _____

CD 4, TR 3

FIRST LISTENING

Listen to the lecture on formal and informal language. As you listen, put the following parts of the lecture in the order that you hear them. Number them 1 to 5.

_____ Differences in vocabulary used in formal and informal language

_____ Tips for a nonnative speaker learning English to learn formal and informal language

_____ Differences in polite phrases used in formal and informal language

_____ Definition and examples of formal language

_____ All languages use different words and phrases in different situations

CD 4, TR 4

SECOND LISTENING

Listen to information from the lecture. The speaker will talk slowly and carefully. You don't have to do anything as you listen. Just relax and listen.

THIRD LISTENING

Listen to the lecture in two parts. Follow the directions for each part. When you have finished, review your notes. Later, you will use them to summarize the lecture with a partner.

Part 1

You will hear the first part of the lecture again. Listen and complete the notes by adding the abbreviations and symbols from the box.

| ex | inform | = | etc. | sits |

Levels of Lang Use
1. All langs — two cats _____ form and inform lvls
   • Diff from correct vs incorrect
   • = diff for diff _____
2. form = txtbks, ref books _____
      ex letter to univ, essays, lectures etc.
      _____ conv w/profs etc
3. _____ lang = conv w/ friends + pers notes etc.

CD 4, TR 5

Part 2

As you listen to the second part of the lecture, take your own notes on a separate piece of paper.

CD 4, TR 6

ACCURACY CHECK

You will hear questions and statements about the lecture. For 1–4, listen to the question and write the letter of the best answer. For 5–8, listen to the statement and write _T_ for _true_ or _F_ for _false_.

_____ 1. a. e-mail to friends
   b. essays
   c. personal notes
   d. text messages

_____ 2. a. family
   b. friends
   c. teammates
   d. all of the above

_____ 3. a. Salt, please.
   b. Pass the salt.
   c. Pass the salt, please.
   d. Could you please pass the salt?

_____ 4. a. I enjoy music.
   b. I saw the cops.
   c. I admire Greek culture.
   d. None of the above

5. _____ 6. _____ 7. _____ 8. _____

ORAL SUMMARY

Use your notes to create an oral summary of the lecture with your partner. As you work together, add details to your notes that your partner included but you had missed.

DISCUSSION

Discuss the following questions with a classmate or in a small group.

1. Is it better to speak formal English in all situations? Why or why not?

2. When you begin learning a second language, should you first learn formal language or informal language? Why?

3. What are some of the ways you think young children learn to use formal and informal language?

4. In what ways do you think it is difficult or easy for second language learners to learn the difference between formal and informal usage?

TASK 1 Homonyms and Homophones

> A *homonym* is a word that is spelled and pronounced the same as another word but has a different meaning, for example *right* (correct) and *right* (opposite of left).
>
> A *homophone* is a word that is spelled differently from another word but pronounced the same, for example *write* and *right*.

🔊 CD 4, TR 7 **A** **Listen to two sentences. One word sounds the same in each sentence. Decide if the word is a *homonym* or a *homophone*, and put a check (✓) in the column. The first one is done for you.**

	Homonym	Homophone
1.	_____	✓
2.	_____	_____
3.	_____	_____
4.	_____	_____
5.	_____	_____
6.	_____	_____
7.	_____	_____
8.	_____	_____
9.	_____	_____

🔊 CD 4, TR 7 **B** **Listen to the sentences again. This time write the two words. The first one is done for you.**

	First sentence	Second sentence
1.	won	one
2.	_____	_____
3.	_____	_____
4.	_____	_____
5.	_____	_____
6.	_____	_____
7.	_____	_____
8.	_____	_____
9.	_____	_____

TASK 2 Classifying Parts of Speech

CD 4, TR 8

Listen to descriptions of the classification of different types of words. As you hear the examples, fill in the charts below.

1.

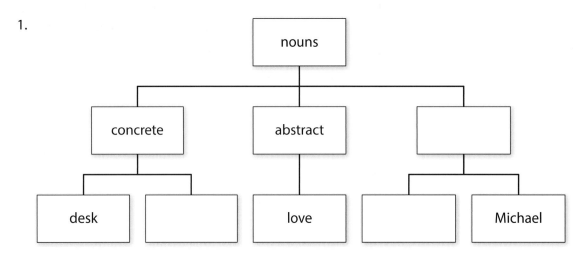

2.

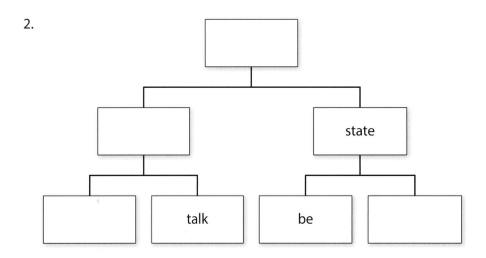

3.

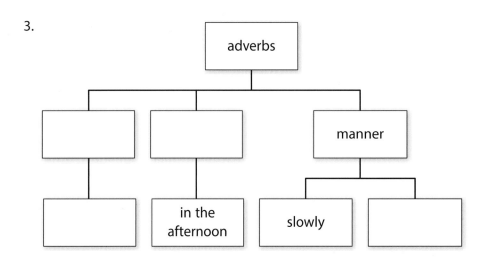

CHAPTER 9

Power

The Kinds of Power People Use and Abuse

TOPIC PREVIEW

Answer the following questions with a partner or your classmates.

1. Who has power over you in your life? What gives these people power?

2. Who do you have power over? What kind of power is it?

3. What gives people power? Some possible sources of power are physical strength, knowledge, wealth, and political influence. Give examples of people you know of who have a lot of each kind of power.

Prince of the Kingdom of Toro, Uganda

VOCABULARY PREVIEW

CD 4, TR 9

A Listen to the following sentences that contain information from the lecture. As you listen, write the word or phrase from the box that completes the sentence.

admires	coercive	expertise	identify with	imitate
legitimate	manipulate	referent	uncomfortable	

1. We all wish to avoid _____ emotions.

2. People who have information can _____ those who do not have this information.

3. Some people may _____ a particular friend or, say, a rock star.

4. Many people _____ and are controlled by the people they identify with.

5. _____ power can be used for good or evil purposes.

6. Often a person _____ or wants to behave like a particular person.

7. Government officials usually exercise _____ power.

8. Some experts use their _____ to gain power.

9. Reward or _____ power is used to reward or punish people's actions or behavior.

B Match the words to their definitions.

_____ 1. legitimate   a. nervous and not relaxed

_____ 2. expertise   b. acceptable and legal

_____ 3. manipulate   c. to make people do what you want, often without them knowing it

_____ 4. admire

_____ 5. referent   d. to like and respect someone

_____ 6. coercive   e. to copy the way someone acts

_____ 7. identify with   f. knowledge and skill

_____ 8. imitate   g. something or someone that you refer to

_____ 9. uncomfortable   h. to feel that you understand and are like another person

                             i. using force to persuade someone to do something

PREDICTIONS

Think about the questions in the Topic Preview on page 63 and the sentences you heard in the Vocabulary Preview. Write three questions that you think will be answered in the lecture. Share your questions with your classmates.

NOTETAKING PREPARATION

Listening for Classifying Language

During a talk or a lecture, a speaker may define a concept by dividing it into various classes or categories. Listen for language that signals that a lecturer is using categories, such as the following:

There are	several two three etc.	categories types kinds sorts classes	of **X**.

X	consists of comprises is made up of	several two three	main	categories. types.

As the lecturer describes each type or category, make sure that you write a number for each new type. Also, leave a space between the notes for each new type.

🔊 CD 4, TR 10 **A** **Listen to five sentences from the lecture. Match the notes below to the information you hear. Write the number of the sentence in the blank.**

_____ P. = 5 cats

_____ 2 more classes of P. – ref & legit

_____ 1st type of P. = inf P.

_____ exp P. = 1+ var of P.

_____ 5th type of P. = reward or coerc P.

Discourse Cues for Definition and Classification   After a lecturer has told you that there are several different kinds of something, listen for the language that tells you that the lecturer is moving from one kind to a new kind.

🔊 CD 4, TR 10 **B** **Listen to sentences that contain information from the lecture. As you listen, write down the missing words from each sentence.**

1. The _____ _____ of power is reward power.

2. _____ _____ of power is referent power.

3. A _____ _____ of power is classified as legitimate power.

4. The _____ _____ of power is expert power.

5. The _____ _____ of power is information power.

CD 4, TR 11

FIRST LISTENING

Listen to the lecture on types of power. As you listen, put the following parts of the lecture in the order that you hear them. Number them 1 to 5.

____ Referent power

____ Reward or coercive power

____ Information power

____ Expert power

____ Legitimate power

CD 4, TR 12

SECOND LISTENING

Listen to information from the lecture. The speaker will talk slowly and carefully. You don't have to do anything as you listen. Just relax and listen.

THIRD LISTENING

Listen to the lecture in two parts. Follow the directions for each part. When you have finished, review your notes. Later, you will use them to summarize the lecture with a partner.

CD 4, TR 13

Part 1

You will hear the first part of the lecture again. Listen and complete the notes by adding the abbreviations and symbols from the box.

e.g.	def	→	legit	5

> **What is Power?**
> 1) _____ = ability to change actions of others
> • prim force of life
> • No P. = uncomfortable feeling
> 2) _____ basic cats
> (1) info P.   (2) ref P.   (3) _____ P.
> (4) expt P.   (5) rew/coerc P.
> 3) Info P.
> • v. eff. contrl
> • ppl w/ info P. can manip. others
> • _____ info in media _____ infl ppl who read it

CD 4, TR 13

Part 2

As you listen to the second part of the lecture, take your own notes on a separate piece of paper.

CD 4, TR 14

ACCURACY CHECK

You will hear questions and statements about the lecture. For 1–4, listen to the question and write the letter of the best answer. For 5–9, listen to the statement and write *T* for *true* or *F* for *false*.

_____ 1. a. reward
      b. referent
      c. legitimate
      d. information

_____ 3. a. coercive
      b. referent
      c. legitimate
      d. information

_____ 2. a. reward
      b. referent
      c. legitimate
      d. information

_____ 4. a. expert
      b. referent
      c. legitimate
      d. information

5. _____   6. _____   7. _____   8. _____   9. _____

ORAL SUMMARY

Use your notes to create an oral summary of the lecture with your partner. As you work together, add details to your notes that your partner included but you had missed.

DISCUSSION

Discuss the following questions with a classmate or in a small group.

1. To some people, power is a game in which winners are powerful, and losers are powerless. Do you agree this statement? Explain why.

2. What types of people have referent power? For example, do rock stars, movie stars, and parents have referent power? Why?

3. Do you agree with the idea that information power is the most effective type of personal power? Explain why.

4. Would you say that governments that use reward or coercive power over their people use this power for good? Can you give any examples?

TASK 1 Classifying Animals

🔊
CD 4, TR 15

A Listen to these definitions of classes of animal. As you listen, complete the chart below.

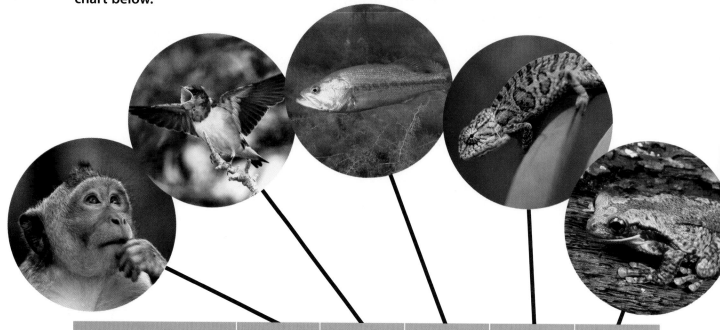

	Mammal	Bird	Fish	Reptile	Amphibian
Warm-blooded	√				
Cold-blooded					
Lives on land	√				
Lives in water	√				
Has two legs and wings					
Has fins					
Gets oxygen from air	√				
Gets oxygen from water					
Starts life in water, but can live on land					
Feeds milk to its young from mother's body	√				
All or most lay eggs					

B Compare your answers with a partner.

TASK 2 What's That Animal?

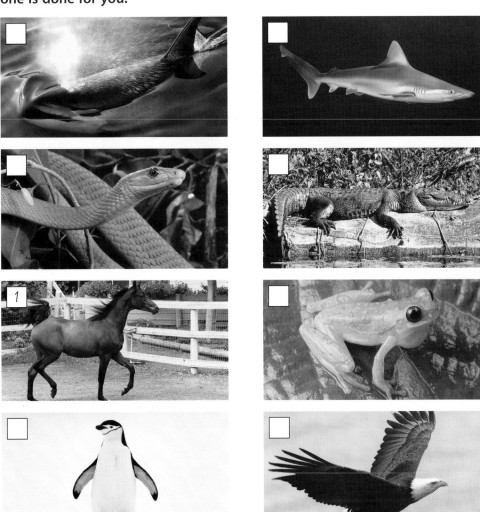

A Listen to descriptions of animals. As you listen, match the description to a picture of the animal and write the number in the box on the picture. The first one is done for you.

B Listen to the name and spelling of each animal and its class, and write them below.

1. Animal: _____horse_____   Class: _____mammal_____

2. Animal: _____   Class: _____

3. Animal: _____   Class: _____

4. Animal: _____   Class: _____

5. Animal: _____   Class: _____

6. Animal: _____   Class: _____

7. Animal: _____   Class: _____

8. Animal: _____   Class: _____

CD 4, TR 16

CD 4, TR 16

People, Plants, and Pollinators

TOPIC PREVIEW

Write down five things that you think about bees. Then compare your list with a classmate's list.

_____

_____

_____

_____

_____

VOCABULARY PREVIEW

A Read the definitions of these key words and phrases that you will hear during the video.

entomologist a scientist who studies insects

originate to come from

migrated in waves moved in large groups from one area to another

diversity the fact of there being many different forms or varieties

gentle having a kind or quiet nature; not violent

species a group of plants or animals that share many similar qualities

beekeeper a person who raises bees

valuable worth a lot of money

pollinate to take pollen from a male plant to a female plant

crops plants that are grown in large quantities by farmers

B Work with a partner and guess whether the following statements are true or false. Write *T* for *true* or *F* for *false*.

_____ 1. Dino Martins is an **entomologist**.

_____ 2. Bees **originated** in South America and then **migrated in waves** to the rest of the world.

_____ 3. There is very little **diversity** in honeybees. They are all very similar.

_____ 4. Honeybees can be very **gentle** insects.

_____ 5. **Beekeepers** only ever keep one **species** of bees at a time.

_____ 6. Some varieties of honey are more **valuable** than others.

_____ 7. **Crops**, such as chocolate and coffee, need insects to **pollinate** them.

VIEWING

🖥 FIRST VIEWING

Watch the video. As you watch, check your answers in **B**, above. Then discuss with a partner why each statement is *true* or *false*.

🖥 SECOND VIEWING

Watch the video again. Listen for the missing words and write them in the blanks.

1. There are two fantastic varieties of honeybee that we get to work with, the lovely mountain honeybee, Monticola, which is a very gentle, _____-colored species and produces lots and lots of _____.

2. And Maria here is a beekeeper, a _____ beekeeper on the slopes of Mount Meru in Tanzania. And you can see a view inside the stingless _____ there.

3. A lot of the work I'm trying to develop right now is managing and _____ stingless bee.

4. He even keeps species that _____ don't know about.

5. If you can spend just _____ minutes a day in the company of an _____, your life will never be the same again.

THIRD VIEWING

Complete these notes as you watch the video. Use abbreviations and symbols.

1) hbs → from E. _____

   hbs in Afr. ↑↑ _____

2) 2 varieties of hb

Monticola	= gentle	_____ -colored	_____
Scutellata	_____	≠ calm	lots of honey

3) Stingless bees
   - In T.
   - 2 _____
   - v. _____ honey

4) Stanley = st b. _____ in Western _____ .
   - keeps _____ species
   - inc. species _____ don't know

5) Crops need _____
   - ex: coffee and _____ .

AFTER VIEWING

ORAL SUMMARY

Use your notes to create an oral summary of the video with your partner. As you work together, add details to your notes that your partner included but you had missed.

DISCUSSION

Discuss the following questions with a classmate or in a small group.

1. How are humans and honeybees similar?

2. What did the woman in the video learn? Why is she surprised? Did this information surprise you, too?

3. Why does Dino Martins ask the audience about chocolate and coffee?

4. Has this video changed your opinion of insects and entomologists? Why or why not?

Comparison and Contrast

Describing Similarities and Differences

A Great Dane and a little Chihuahua

Asian and African Elephants

Similarities and Differences

TOPIC PREVIEW

Answer the following questions with a partner or your classmates.

1. Discuss the animals you see in the photo on this page. What do you know about these animals?

2. Have you ever seen a real elephant? Describe where and when you saw it. What impressed you most about the animal?

3. Talk about the similarities and differences between elephants (the largest animals that live on land) and whales (the largest animals that live in water).

A young elephant in Kaziranga National Park, India

VOCABULARY PREVIEW

CD 5, TR 1

A **Listen to the following sentences that contain information from the lecture. As you listen, write the word from the box that completes the sentence.**

enormous	fascinating	mammals	tamer	temperament
trained	trunk	tusks	wilder	

1. Today's topic is the largest land _____ on earth—elephants.

2. Elephants are _____ animals.

3. An elephant uses its _____ to put grasses, leaves, and water into its mouth.

4. Elephants can be _____ to do heavy work.

5. The Asian elephant sometimes does not have any _____ at all.

6. A big difference between the two types of elephants is their _____.

7. The Asian elephant is _____ than the African elephant.

8. The African elephant is much _____ than the Asian elephant.

9. There certainly are differences between the African and the Asian elephants, but they are both _____ animals.

B **Match the words to their definitions.**

_____ 1. mammal   a. the long nose of an elephant

_____ 2. enormous   b. to teach to do something

_____ 3. fascinating   c. easy for people to control and teach

_____ 4. tame   d. one of the two long teeth that an elephant has

_____ 5. temperament e. very difficult for people to control

_____ 6. train   f. of very great or large size; huge

_____ 7. trunk   g. very interesting

_____ 8. tusk   h. nature; outlook; personality

_____ 9. wild   i. an animal that feeds its own milk to its babies

PREDICTIONS

Think about the questions in the Topic Preview on page 74 and the sentences you heard in the Vocabulary Preview. Write three questions that you think will be answered in the lecture. Share your questions with your classmates.

NOTETAKING PREPARATION

Making a Comparison Chart

As soon as a lecturer indicates that he or she is going to compare or contrast two things, a good notetaker will make a chart with two columns and put the name of the two things that are going to be compared at the top of the columns.

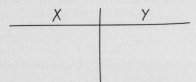

Listen for statements such as

There are two types of
*Today I am going to be talking about **X** and **Y***
*Today's lecture will compare and contrast **X** and **Y***

A well-planned lecture will compare each point in an organized way so that you can list each of the points opposite each other in the chart. When something is the same on both sides of the chart, you can save time by just putting a check (✔) in the second column.

CD 5, TR 2

A **Listen to this short talk about two types of camels. As you listen, make a chart below and write in some details about each kind of camel.**

Discourse Cues for Comparison and Contrast   Listen for language that indicates that the lecturer is making a comparison. Key words and phrases to listen for are:

*Both **X** and **Y** . . .*
*One/another similarity is that **X** and **Y** . . .*
***X** and **Y** are alike in that . . .*

CD 5, TR 2

B **Listen to part of the lecture. As you listen, count the number of times that the lecturer uses the word *both*. Circle your answer below.**

    a. 2   b. 3   c. 4   d. 5

FIRST LISTENING

CD 5, TR 3

Listen to the lecture on elephants. As you listen, put the following parts of the lecture in the order that you hear them. Number them 1 to 5.

_____ The continents elephants come from

_____ Elephants' temperaments

_____ Elephants' trunks

_____ Elephants' size

_____ Elephants' intelligence

SECOND LISTENING

CD 5, TR 4

Listen to information from the lecture. The speaker will talk slowly and carefully. You don't have to do anything as you listen. Just relax and listen.

THIRD LISTENING

Listen to the lecture in two parts. Follow the directions for each part. When you have finished, review your notes. Later, you will use them to summarize the lecture with a partner.

Part 1

CD 5, TR 5

You will hear the first part of the lecture again. Listen and complete the notes by adding the abbreviations and symbols from the box.

√	e.g.	gals	+	Afr.

	Asian E	_____ E
has trunk		√
eats leaves + grass		
picks up obj _____ trees		
drinks 50 _____ H_2O per day		_____
intellgnt		√
heavy work		
do tricks _____ entertain		

Part 2

CD 5, TR 5

As you listen to the second part of the lecture, take your own notes on a separate piece of paper.

ACCURACY CHECK

🔊 **(A)** **You will hear four questions about the lecture. Listen to each question and write the letter of the best answer.**
CD 5, TR 6

_____ 1. a. ear
b. trunk
c. tooth
d. tusk

_____ 2. a. African elephants
b. Asian elephants
c. both Asian and African
d. neither African nor Asian

_____ 3. a. 7,000 to 12,000 lbs.
b. 8,000 to 10,000 lbs.
c. 12,000 to 14,000 lbs.
d. 18,000 to 20,000 lbs.

_____ 4. a. larger and lighter
b. heavier and larger
c. lighter and smaller
d. smaller and heavier

🔊 **(B)** **You will hear five statements about the lecture. Listen to each statement and decide if you heard the information in the lecture. Write Y for yes or N for no.**
CD 5, TR 6

1. _____   2. _____   3. _____   4. _____   5. _____

ORAL SUMMARY

Use your notes to create an oral summary of the lecture with your partner. As you work together, add details to your notes that your partner included but you had missed.

DISCUSSION

Discuss the following questions with a classmate or in a small group.

1. Some people say the one animal that doesn't belong in a zoo is the elephant. Do you agree? Why? Do you think there are animals other than elephants that don't belong in zoos or circuses?

2. Compare two domestic animals (dog, cat, horse, etc.) and two wild animals (giraffe, bear, wolf, etc.). How are the two domestic animals similar and different? How are the two wild animals similar and different?

3. Some Asian elephants are working animals that are trained to do work such as lifting tree trunks for people. What animals do work in your country? What work do they do?

4. How are the kinds of pets sold in pet stores and those given away by animal rescue organizations such as the ASPCA similar or different?

TASK 1 The Hippo and the Rhino

A Listen to the talk about the similarities and differences between the hippopotamus—the hippo—and the rhinoceros—the rhino. As you listen, complete the Venn diagram with the information below.

CD 5, TR 7

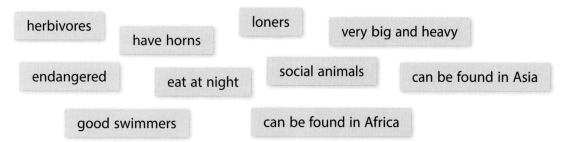

herbivores   loners   very big and heavy
have horns
endangered   eat at night   social animals   can be found in Asia
good swimmers   can be found in Africa

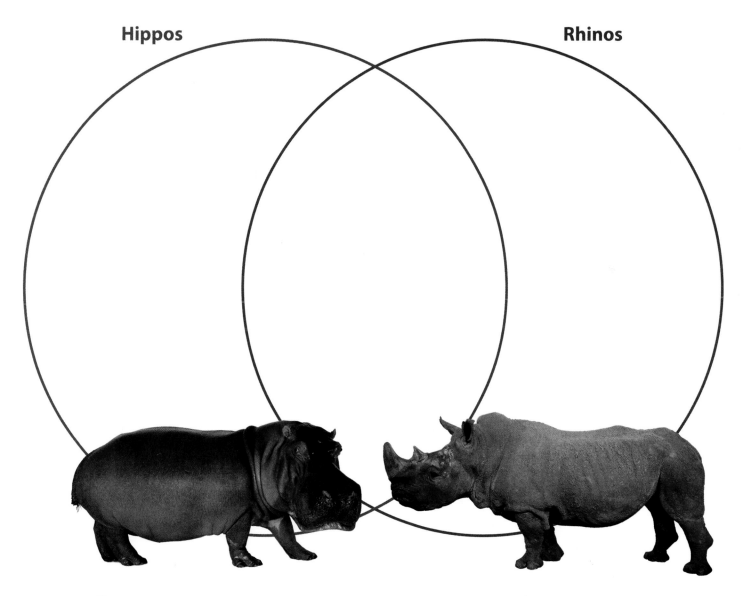

Hippos   **Rhinos**

B Compare your answers with a partner and make sentences that compare and contrast the two animals.

TASK 2 Two Brothers

CD 5, TR 8

A Listen for similarities and differences between two brothers, Charlie and David. As you listen, put a check (✓) in the correct box under each picture.

Charlie		David
☐	is married	☐
☐	has two children	☐
☐	has a girl and a boy	☐
☐	works in an office	☐
☐	works as a firefighter	☐
☐	likes jazz music	☐
☐	likes to play golf	☐
☐	is wealthy	☐

B Compare your answers with a partner.

CHAPTER 11

Lincoln and Kennedy

Different Times, Similar Destinies

TOPIC PREVIEW

Answer the following questions with a partner or your classmates.

1. What do you know about Abraham Lincoln and John F. Kennedy? Talk about how you think the two men are similar and how they are different.

2. Do you know when Lincoln or Kennedy lived? What was happening in the United States at those times?

3. Both men met a sad end. Do you know what it was? Can you describe what happened to each man?

John F. Kennedy

Abraham Lincoln, Lincoln Memorial, Washington, DC

VOCABULARY PREVIEW

CD 5, TR 9

A **Listen to the following sentences that contain information from the lecture. As you listen, write the word from the box that completes the sentence.**

assassinated	career	coincidences	demonstrations	elected
fates	formal	rights	term	

1. I'll say a few words about Lincoln's and Kennedy's tragic _____.

2. Both Lincoln and Kennedy were _____ while in office.

3. In spite of his lack of _____ education, Lincoln became a well-known lawyer.

4. Books have been written about the strange _____ in the lives of the two men.

5. Lincoln began his political _____ in Congress.

6. Lincoln and Kennedy were _____ to Congress 100 years apart.

7. At the time Kennedy took office, African Americans were being denied their civil _____.

8. Unrest took the form of civil rights _____.

9. Neither president lived to complete his _____ in office.

B **Match the words with their definitions.**

_____ 1. assassinate a. a set length of time for something, from start to finish

_____ 2. right b. the things that happen to someone

_____ 3. coincidence c. usual or official

_____ 4. career d. a person's work

_____ 5. demonstration e. something such as equality that all people have

_____ 6. elect f. a public march or gathering when people show they are for or against something

_____ 7. fate

_____ 8. formal g. to kill an important person, often for a political reason

_____ 9. term h. the surprising way two similar things happen

i. to choose someone by voting

PREDICTIONS

Think about the questions in the Topic Preview on page 81 and the sentences you heard in the Vocabulary Preview. Write three questions that you think will be answered in the lecture. Share your questions with your classmates.

NOTETAKING PREPARATION

Listening to the Lecture Overview

A good lecturer will very often begin the lecture by providing students with an overview of what will be talked about and in what order. Listen carefully to this overview and try to quickly write down and number the different sections of the lecture. As you listen to the rest of the lecture, use those numbers as the lecturer starts each new section.

The overview will very often contain language such as

First, I'm going to talk about . . .   *I'll also be talking about . . .*
Then I'll tell you . . .   *Finally, I'll end by . . .*

CD 5, TR 10

A You will hear the beginnings of two lectures about U.S. presidents. Listen to the lecturer give an overview of lecture 1 and then of lecture 2. As you listen, write down and number the main sections of each lecture on the notepaper below.

1.

2.

Discourse Cues for Comparison and Contrast
Listen for language cues that show that a lecturer is making or is going to make a contrast such as the following:

however   *one/another difference is*
whereas   *on the other hand*
while   *in contrast*

CD 5, TR 10

B Listen to five sentences that contain information from the lecture. As you listen to each sentence, write the language cue you hear the lecturer use to make a contrast.

1. _____

2. _____

3. _____

4. _____

5. _____

CD 5, TR 11

FIRST LISTENING

Listen to the lecture on Presidents Lincoln and Kennedy. As you listen, put the following parts of the lecture in the order that you hear them. Number them 1 to 5.

_____ Some coincidences in the lives of the two presidents

_____ The lecturer's personal memory of the death of President Kennedy

_____ Where the presidents were educated

_____ When the presidents were born

_____ The circumstances of the presidents' assassinations

CD 5, TR 12

SECOND LISTENING

Listen to information from the lecture. The speaker will talk slowly and carefully. You don't have to do anything as you listen. Just relax and listen.

THIRD LISTENING

Listen to the lecture in two parts. Follow the directions for each part. When you have finished, review your notes. Later, you will use them to summarize the lecture with a partner.

CD 5, TR 13

Part 1

You will hear the first part of the lecture again. Listen and complete the notes by adding the abbreviations and symbols from the box.

fam	ed	c	Polit.	b.

Overview
1. Diffs   2. Fam. lives   3. _____ lives   4. Trag. fates

Kennedy	Lincoln
20 _____	19c
b. 1917	_____ 1809
rich _____	not rich
exp. schools + Harvard	1 yr of form ed
	self _____ man

CD 5, TR 13

Part 2

As you listen to the second part of the lecture, take your own notes on a separate piece of paper.

ACCURACY CHECK

CD 5, TR 14

You will hear 10 questions about the lecture. Write a short answer to each question. Use your notes.

1. _____
2. _____
3. _____
4. _____
5. _____
6. _____
7. _____
8. _____
9. _____
10. _____

ORAL SUMMARY

Use your notes to create an oral summary of the lecture with your partner. As you work together, add details to your notes that your partner included but you had missed.

DISCUSSION

Discuss the following questions with a classmate or in a small group.

1. Read the quotations below. What do they mean to you?

    A house divided against itself can not stand. —Abraham Lincoln

    Ask not what your country can do for you, ask what you can do for your country. —John F. Kennedy

2. There have been conflicting theories about the assassination of John F. Kennedy: the "lone assassin" theory and the "conspiracy" theory. Do you know what these theories are? Explain what you think they mean.

3. What do the following statements say about how people "rally around," or support, their leaders during times of crisis? Explain.

    Kennedy's highest approval rating as president came right after the disastrous invasion of Cuba at the Bay of Pigs.

    President George H. W. Bush experienced his highest levels of popular support at the time of the Gulf War.

TASK 1 Two First Ladies

Mrs. Jacqueline Bouvier Kennedy,
wife of President John F. Kennedy

Mrs. Mary Todd Lincoln,
wife of President Abraham Lincoln

CD 5, TR 15

Listen to five similarities between the wives of President Lincoln and President Kennedy. You will hear each similarity twice. Write below exactly what you hear.

1. _____

2. _____

3. _____

4. _____

5. _____

TASK 2 Two Vice Presidents

Vice President Lyndon Johnson,
President Kennedy's vice president

Vice President Andrew Johnson,
President Lincoln's vice president

CD 5, TR 16

A **Listen to these interesting differences and similarities between Kennedy's vice president, Lyndon Johnson, and Lincoln's vice president, Andrew Johnson. Circle** *similarity* **if you hear a similarity or** *difference* **if you hear difference.**

1. SIMILARITY   DIFFERENCE   5. SIMILARITY   DIFFERENCE

2. SIMILARITY   DIFFERENCE   6. SIMILARITY   DIFFERENCE

3. SIMILARITY   DIFFERENCE   7. SIMILARITY   DIFFERENCE

4. SIMILARITY   DIFFERENCE

CD 5, TR 16

B **Listen again to the statements about the two vice presidents. Take notes about each similarity or difference.**

1. _____

2. _____

3. _____

4. _____

5. _____

6. _____

7. _____

C **Compare your notes with a partner and check to see if you circled the correct word,** *similarity* **or** *difference*, **in A above.**

CHAPTER

12

The *Titanic* and the *Costa Concordia*

Tragedies at Sea

TOPIC PREVIEW

Answer the following questions with a partner or a classmate.

1. Describe the picture on this page. What do you think is happening?

2. Have you ever seen a movie or a video about the sinking of a ship? What was the name of the movie? What was the story like? What did you like or dislike about the movie?

3. What do you expect to find on the ship if you decide to take a vacation cruise?

The Italian cruise ship *Costa Concordia*, on the rocks, January 2012

VOCABULARY PREVIEW

CD 6, TR 1

A Listen to the following sentences that contain information from the lecture. As you listen, write the word or phrase from the box that completes the sentence.

courage	cowardice	disasters	iceberg	lifeboats
partial	set sail	shelf	sink	

1. On the morning of April 10, 1912, the *Titanic* _____ from England.

2. Reports of the sinking—or the _____ sinking—of the *Costa Concordia* filled the newspapers, television, and the Internet for days.

3. As each ship was sinking, there were acts of _____.

4. Some men on the *Titanic* gave up their seats in the _____ to women and children.

5. So, on the *Costa Concordia*, there were also acts of courage and acts of _____.

6. I'd like to point out some of the big differences between these two ship _____.

7. Another difference was what caused these ships to _____.

8. The *Titanic* struck an _____.

9. The *Costa Concordia* struck a _____ of rocks near an island.

B Match the words to their definitions.

_____ 1. courage

_____ 2. iceberg

_____ 3. set sail

_____ 4. lifeboat

_____ 5. cowardice

_____ 6. sink

_____ 7. partial

_____ 8. shelf

_____ 9. disaster

a. not complete or not entirely

b. fear and a lack of ability to help in a dangerous situation

c. an event that causes a lot of damage and injury

d. the ability to overcome fear when there is danger

e. a long, flat area of rock under the water

f. to begin a trip on a boat or ship

g. a large piece of ice that is floating in the ocean

h. to fall under water

i. a boat used to rescue people from ships in trouble

PREDICTIONS

Think about the questions in the Topic Preview on page 88 and the sentences you heard in the Vocabulary Preview. Write three questions that you think will be answered in the lecture. Share your questions with your classmates.

NOTETAKING PREPARATION

Making Your Notes Complete

It is very difficult to take complete notes. Sometimes you can't hear or you miss some information. Sometimes you don't understand what the lecturer just said. And sometimes your mind wanders and you simply stop listening for a few seconds.

When these things happen, do the following:

- Make sure that you leave a space in your notes so that you can come back later and fill in missing information. Put a question mark in or next to the space.

- Arrange to meet after class with some classmates. Ask everyone to share their notes so that as a group you can fill in each other's missing information.

- Ask the lecturer for the information that you missed when the lecture is finished.

CD 6, TR 2

A The notes to the right are incomplete. Listen to a conversation between the notetaker, Alicia, and a classmate, Carlos, and fill in the notes with the missing information that Carlos provides.

> 1) On C.C. acts of courage and cow ?
> - ev man for himself
> - capt of C.C. left ship   ?
>
> ?
>
> - many think capt – leave ship last
> - capt of T. died
> - capt of C.C.   ?

Discourse Cues for Comparison and Contrast When a lecturer is comparing and contrasting two things, listen for discourse cues that tell you if the lecturer is expressing a similarity or a difference.

CD 6, TR 2

B Listen to sentences that contain information from the lecture. As you listen, write the missing words from each sentence in the blanks.

1. _____ the *Titanic* and the *Concordia* were enormous luxury ships.

2. The *Titanic* struck an iceberg, _____ the *Costa Concordia* struck rocks.

3. Another _____ is that as each ship was sinking there were acts of great courage.

4. There were not enough lifeboats on the *Titanic*. _____ _____, there were plenty of lifeboats on the *Costa Concordia*.

5. People lost their lives on the *Concordia*; _____, there was much greater loss of life on the *Titanic*.

FIRST LISTENING

CD 6, TR 3

Listen to the lecture on the sinking of two ships. As you listen, put the following parts of the lecture in the order that you hear them. Number them 1 to 5.

_____ Acts of courage and cowardice aboard the two ships

_____ The size of the ships

_____ The number of people who died and survived

_____ The general safety of traveling

_____ Where and why the ships went down

SECOND LISTENING

CD 6, TR 4

Listen to information from the lecture. The speaker will talk slowly and carefully. You don't have to do anything as you listen. Just relax and listen.

THIRD LISTENING

Listen to the lecture in two parts. Follow the directions for each part. When you have finished, review your notes. Later, you will use them to summarize the lecture with a partner.

Part 1

CD 6, TR 5

You will hear the first part of the lecture again. Listen and complete the notes by adding the abbreviations and symbols from the box.

lux	enorm	1st	+	3)

Titanic sail Apr 10, 1912   Costa Concordia — ? 2012

Similarities

1) Both _____

   T. — 882 ft + 9 decks

   C.C. — 951 ft _____ 13 decks

2) Both _____ ships

   Pools, restaurants etc.

   _____ On both ships acts of courag and coward

   On T. — men let women + child. _____

   But . . . one man dressed as woman

Part 2

CD 6, TR 5

As you listen to the second part of the lecture, take your own notes on a separate piece of paper.

ACCURACY CHECK

CD 6, TR 6

A You will hear eight questions about the lecture. Listen to each question and write the letter of the best answer.

_____ 1. a. January 13, 1910
b. January 13, 2012
c. April 10, 1912
d. April 10, 2012

_____ 2. a. England
b. Italy
c. the United States
d. none of the above

_____ 3. a. Both were over 880 feet long.
b. Both were luxury liners.
c. Both sank in deep water.
d. Both sailed to Italy.

_____ 4. a. *Titanic* sank in shallow water.
b. *Titanic* was the taller ship.
c. *Costa Concordia* hit rocks.
d. *Costa Concordia* was small.

_____ 5. a. the *Titanic*
b. the *Costa Concordia*
c. both a and b
d. none of the above

_____ 6. a. 25
b. 32
c. 700
d. 1,500

_____ 7. a. It struck an iceberg.
b. It struck a shelf of rocks.
c. It ran into another ship.
d. It had enough lifeboats.

_____ 8. a. Accidents can happen.
b. Disaster is possible.
c. Most ships arrive safely.
d. all of the above

CD 6, TR 6

B You will hear six statements about the lecture. Listen to each statement and decide if it mentions a similarity or a difference. Write *S* for *similarity* or *D* for *difference*.

1. _____   2. _____   3. _____   4. _____   5. _____   6. _____

ORAL SUMMARY

Use your notes to create an oral summary of the lecture with your partner. As you work together, add details to your notes that your partner included but you had missed.

DISCUSSION

Discuss the following questions with a classmate or in a small group.

1. Compare how you travel within your country to how you travel between countries. Do you travel by plane, train, car, ship, or another way? Why?

2. What do you think you would enjoy doing if you went on a cruise? What would you not like to do on a cruise? Explain.

3. Compare and contrast two transportation disasters that happened in your country or somewhere else. What happened? What was the result of these tragedies?

CD 6, TR 7

TASK 1 The Hindenburg Disaster

Listen to sentences comparing the 1937 *Hindenburg* disaster with the 1912 *Titanic* disaster. As you listen, write missing words in the blanks to complete the sentences.

1. The *Hindenburg* and the *Titanic* were both _____ passenger ships. The _____ was that one of them was an airship and the other was an _____ liner.

2. _____ vessels created a lot of excitement among the general _____. They both represented the beginning of a new era of luxury _____.

3. The *Titanic* sank on its maiden voyage after hitting an iceberg. The *Hindenburg*, on the other _____, caught fire and crashed on its _____ voyage.

4. Like the *Titanic*, there were _____ from the *Hindenburg* crash. Of the 97 people on board the *Hindenburg*, 35 people died and _____ survived.

5. No news crews _____ the sinking of the *Titanic*. However, the crash of the *Hindenburg* was _____. One reporter, Herbert Morrison, gave a breathless account that millions listened to on the _____.

CD 6, TR 8

TASK 2 Easily Confused Words

Listen to descriptions of some easily confused words. Write the word you hear next to its correct description.

1. _____ : many people like you

   _____ : many people know about you

2. _____ : very well-known

   _____ : well-known because of doing something bad

3. _____ : unpopular, and feeling bad about it

   _____ : not with other people

4. _____ : not many

   _____ : describing a small but positive number

Free Soloing with Alex Honnold

TOPIC PREVIEW

Work with a partner to make a list or draw pictures in the box below. Draw or list the different pieces of equipment mountain climbers use to keep them safe when they climb.

VOCABULARY PREVIEW

A Read the definitions of these key words and phrases that you will hear during the video.

gear special equipment used to do a particular activity or sport

at the top of [this] game at the very highest level of ability

unbelievably gifted with an amazing, incredible natural talent

revolves around turns in a circle about a central point that is the focus

memorable moments times that are so enjoyable or important in your life that you expect you will always remember them

switched changed

well within his ability something that he could easily do

awesome amazing, extraordinary, fantastic, wonderful

B Work with a partner and discuss answers to the following questions.

1. Is there anything that is **well within your ability** to do but not easy for other people that you know?

2. Does your life **revolve around** a particular person, place, or activity?

3. In what areas can some people be **unbelievably gifted**?

4. What special **gear** do you need to do an activity that you enjoy doing?

5. Describe a time when you decided to stop doing something and to **switch** and do something different.

6. At what age do you think you were **at the top of your game**?

7. What experiences have you had that you would describe as "**awesome**" or "**memorable moments**"?

VIEWING

FIRST VIEWING

Watch the video, and then compare your first impressions with a partner. Talk about what you remember, what surprised you, and what interested you.

SECOND VIEWING

Watch the video again. Listen for the missing words and write them in the blanks.

1. Free soloing has to be the ultimate in free _____.

2. The reason it's probably the ultimate is because one _____ move, you fall, you die.

3. Yeah, I would say that Yosemite probably is the _____ of my climbing.

Half Dome, Yosemite National Park

4. For most people on this planet who are serious climbers, doing Half Dome in a day or two is considered _____. Alex did it in three hours, without a _____.

5. I've sort of embraced the whole _____, you know, embraced the unpleasant parts, too.

Complete these notes as you watch the video. Write only important words, not full sentences, and abbreviate common words.

1) Free soloing
   FS = ultim _____
   FS = w/o _____, _____, pwr of _____
       w/ _____, _____, chalk _____
       _____ → death

2) Yosemite – ctr of climbing
   • _____
   • _____
   • Half Dome – _____

3) Tired/stalled out
   • _____
   • _____

4) Last season
   • _____
   • _____
   • Awesome!

AFTER VIEWING

ORAL SUMMARY

Use your notes to create an oral summary of the video with your partner. As you work together, add details to your notes that your partner included but you had missed.

DISCUSSION

Discuss the following questions with a classmate or in a small group.

1. Why does the narrator, Jenkins, say that Alex Honnold is "like Michael Jordan"?

2. How is free soloing different from how most climbers climb?

3. What is something you have done to "stretch your limits," that is, something that is physically difficult and challenging for you?

Cause and Effect

Describing the Reason Things Happen

Polar bear surrounded by
melting Arctic pack ice

Dinosaurs

Why They Disappeared

TOPIC PREVIEW

Answer the following questions with a partner or your classmates.

1. Only the bones of the dinosaurs can be seen today, mainly in museums. Have you ever seen the bones of a dinosaur? Describe when and where you saw them. If you haven't seen any, would you like to see dinosaur bones? Why?

2. Describe what a *Tyrannosaurus rex* or another type of dinosaur probably looked like. When did this dinosaur live on earth, how large was it, and what was its food?

3. What is climate change? Do we feel the influence of climate change today? Why or why not?

Dinosaur skeletons on display at the National Museum of Natural History, Leiden, The Netherlands

VOCABULARY PREVIEW

CD 6, TR 9

A **Listen to the following sentences that contain information from the lecture. As you listen, write the word or phrase from the box that completes the sentence.**

asteroid	blocked out	died out	debate	element
extinct	gradual	shortage	speculate	

1. Scientists suggest several theories for why dinosaurs became _____.

2. Perhaps one day we will know for certain why dinosaurs such as the *Tyrannosaurus rex* _____.

3. We continue to _____ and to search for why dinosaurs disappeared.

4. The change in climate caused a severe _____ of food.

5. Many scientists believe that _____ climate change best explains why the dinosaurs disappeared.

6. The second theory suggests that a huge _____ hit the earth 65 million years ago when the dinosaurs still walked the earth.

7. The enormous dust cloud covered the whole earth and _____ the sun for months and months.

8. Iridium is an _____ that is not common on earth.

9. Today scientists continue to _____ these two theories and others, too.

B **Match the words to their definitions.**

_____ 1. die out   a. to make guesses about something

_____ 2. speculate   b. not existing any longer

_____ 3. gradual   c. to slowly disappear over time and stop existing

_____ 4. element   d. to talk about the different ideas about something

_____ 5. debate   e. a rock moving through outer space

_____ 6. extinct   f. to prevent light or sound from reaching somewhere

_____ 7. asteroid   g. a situation where there is too little of something

_____ 8. block out   h. little by little; happening very, very slowly

_____ 9. shortage   i. a substance that cannot be broken down into smaller parts

PREDICTIONS

Think about the questions in the Topic Preview on page 98 and the sentences you heard in the Vocabulary Preview. Write three questions that you think will be answered in the lecture. Share your questions with your classmates.

NOTETAKING PREPARATION

Using Arrows for Cause and Effect

You learned in Chapter 2 that arrows are very useful symbols. When a lecturer describes the causes and effect of events, use arrows in your notes to show what is the cause and what is the effect by the direction the arrow points. The arrow should always point to the effect.

You hear	You write
X causes Y	X → Y
X is the result of Y	X ← Y

CD 6, TR 10

A Listen to the following causes and effects described in the lecture. Use either →
or ← to complete the notes below.

1. Dinos extinct _____ plnt clim change

2. Clim cooler _____ dinos disapp

3. Ast hit earth _____ v. big cloud dust

4. Food vanish _____ dinos too

5. Perhps find dinos die _____ disease

Discourse Cues for Causal Analysis   Listen for language cues that indicate that the lecturer is describing causes and effects.

Verbs	Nouns	Transitions	Conjunctions
cause	cause	therefore	because (of)
result in/from	result	as a result (of)	since
lead to	reason	for this reason	so

CD 6, TR 10

B Listen to the sentences in **A** again. As you listen, write the complete sentences below.

1. Dinosaurs became extinct _____.

2. The climate of the world became cooler. _____.

3. When the asteroid hit the earth, _____.

4. Their food vanished, _____.

5. Perhaps they'll find out that dinosaurs died out _____.

FIRST LISTENING

CD 6, TR 11

Listen to the lecture about dinosaurs. As you listen, put the following parts of the lecture in the order that you hear them. Number them 1 to 5.

_____ The asteroid impact theory

_____ Possible other theories

_____ The climate change theory

_____ Two different theories that some scientists believe today

_____ Iridium in earth as evidence of asteroid theory

SECOND LISTENING

CD 6, TR 12

Listen to information from the lecture. The speaker will talk slowly and carefully. You don't have to do anything as you listen. Just relax and listen.

THIRD LISTENING

Listen to the lecture in two parts. Follow the directions for each part. When you have finished, review your notes. Later, you will use them to summarize the lecture with a partner.

CD 6, TR 13

Part 1

You will hear the first part of the lecture again. Listen and complete the notes by adding the abbreviations and symbols from the box.

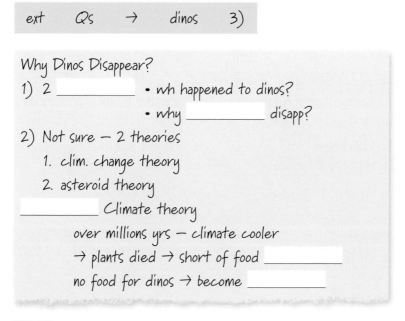

ext   Qs   →   dinos   3)

Why Dinos Disappear?
1) 2 _____ • wh happened to dinos?
                • why _____ disapp?
2) Not sure — 2 theories
   1. clim. change theory
   2. asteroid theory
_____ Climate theory
   over millions yrs — climate cooler
   → plants died → short of food _____
   no food for dinos → become _____

CD 6, TR 13

Part 2

As you listen to the second part of the lecture, take your own notes on a separate piece of paper.

ACCURACY CHECK

CD 6, TR 14

A You will hear five questions about the lecture. Write a short answer to each question. Use your notes.

1. _____

2. _____

3. _____

4. _____

5. _____

CD 6, TR 14

B You will hear five statements about the lecture. Listen to each statement and write *T* for *true* or *F* for *false*.

1. _____   2. _____   3. _____   4. _____   5. _____

ORAL SUMMARY

Use your notes to create an oral summary of the lecture with your partner. As you work together, add details to your notes that your partner included but you had missed.

DISCUSSION

Discuss the following questions with a classmate or in a small group.

1. Which of the two theories, the asteroid impact theory or the gradual climate-change theory, do you think best explains the disappearance of the dinosaurs?

2. What do you suggest as another theory for why the dinosaurs disappeared? Use your imagination to come up with some possible causes.

3. What are the names of some dinosaurs you are familiar with? Draw a picture of a dinosaur as you picture it in your mind. Describe what it is doing in your picture.

4. Some scientists think today's birds and perhaps some lizards, such as the Komodo dragon, are descendants of the dinosaurs of the past. Do you agree? Why or why not?

TASK 1 What's the Reason?

CD 6, TR 15

A **Listen to the situations. As you listen, decide if a, b, c, or d is the cause. Circle your answer.**

1. a. You are sitting too close to it.
   b. The set isn't plugged in.
   c. You forgot to pay your telephone bill.
   d. You forgot to pay your electricity bill.

2. a. The park is near her house.
   b. Her best friend is going to be there.
   c. The weather is warm and sunny.
   d. She has to study for an exam.

3. a. He often gave too much money to customers by mistake.
   b. He found a new job immediately.
   c. He was sometimes rude to the customers.
   d. He doesn't have enough money to pay his bills.

4. a. His grandmother was French.
   b. He liked living in Paris.
   c. He went to Paris to get a job.
   d. His parents lived there in the 1970s.

5. a. The teacher didn't like Antonia.
   b. The examination was very easy.
   c. The examination was too difficult for the class.
   d. Antonia didn't understand the directions for the test.

6. a. Your doctor is out of town.
   b. You can't find your phone.
   c. The doctor's office is very busy when you call.
   d. The doctor's phone is out of order.

7. a. Tony was very unlucky.
   b. It's very expensive to fly to Monte Carlo.
   c. Tony doesn't have enough money to get home.
   d. Tony doesn't like to lose money when he gambles.

8. a. He is a soccer player.
   b. He has just finished playing tennis.
   c. His wife is getting ready to play tennis.
   d. He is going to play volleyball.

B **Compare your answers with a partner.**

TASK 2 You Write the Ending

A Listen to five unfinished stories. Take notes about what happens.

1. It's a cold and snowy night.

2. It's the second half of a championship soccer game.

3. A fisherman is walking by the side of the river.

4. You and your friend are sitting in the movie theater watching a movie.

5. A man is crossing a street in New York.

B Look at your notes and create an ending for each story. Tell your ending to the stories to a classmate.

CHAPTER

14

The U.S. Civil War

Why It Happened

TOPIC PREVIEW

Answer the following questions with a partner or your classmates.

1. What is a civil war? What kinds of situations can cause a civil war to happen? Name a civil war that happened in the past and briefly talk about the causes and results of this civil war.

2. What do you know about the U.S. Civil War? What caused this war? What role did slavery play in the war?

3. What do you know about Abraham Lincoln and his role in the U.S. Civil War?

Painting showing the Battle of Gettysburg, 1863

VOCABULARY PREVIEW

CD 7, TR 1

A Listen to the following sentences that contain information from the lecture. As you listen, write the word or phrase from the box that completes the sentence.

descendant	devastation	dominate	foundation	plantations
secede	tension	vital	way of life	

1. I'm a _____ of a soldier who fought for the Union—that is, the North—in the Civil War.

2. There were a number of reasons for _____ between the North and the South.

3. Slavery was, in fact, the _____ of the economy in the South.

4. In the South there were large _____ that grew cotton and tobacco.

5. Many Southerners feared that the North would _____ the country.

6. When Abraham Lincoln became President of the United States, the South decided it was time to _____ from the Union.

7. The people of the South were afraid that their _____ was in danger.

8. The Civil War led to the _____ of the South.

9. The South today is a _____ part of these United States.

B Match the words to their definitions.

_____ 1. tension   a. very important; necessary

_____ 2. devastation   b. a child or relative of someone who lived in the past

_____ 3. foundation   c. to leave a group, organization, or country

_____ 4. dominate   d. a large farm where a particular crop is grown to be sold

_____ 5. secede   e. an anxious feeling when people don't trust each other

_____ 6. way of life   f. the usual way a person or a group of people lives

_____ 7. descendant   g. serious damage caused to a people, area, or country

_____ 8. vital   h. the part on which other parts rest or depend for support

_____ 9. plantation   i. to control or rule by strength or power

PREDICTIONS

Think about the questions in the Topic Preview on page 105 and the sentences you heard in the Vocabulary Preview. Write three questions that you think will be answered in the lecture. Share your questions with your classmates.

NOTETAKING PREPARATION

When Not to Take Notes

It's not always necessary to take notes on everything a lecturer says. For example, the lecturer may tell a personal story or give information that is not directly related to the main points of the lecture. When the lecturer starts to do that, you don't need to take notes.

CD 7, TR 2

A **Listen to parts of the lecture on the causes of the U.S. Civil War. Decide if you need to take notes on those parts or don't need to take notes. Circle your answers, a or b.**

1. a. need to take notes   b. don't need to take notes

2. a. need to take notes   b. don't need to take notes

3. a. need to take notes   b. don't need to take notes

4. a. need to take notes   b. don't need to take notes

5. a. need to take notes   b. don't need to take notes

6. a. need to take notes   b. don't need to take notes

Discourse Cues for Causal Analysis In academic classes, lectures don't just describe what happened and when. A good lecturer will analyze events and help students think about why things happened. As the lecturer discusses causes, he or she will use certain discourse cues. Make sure that you learn these and can recognize when the lecturer has moved from describing to analyzing.

For a list of discourse cues see page 100.

CD 7, TR 2

B **Listen to sentences that contain information from the lecture. As you listen to each sentence, write the words and phrases that the lecturer uses to discuss cause and effect.**

1. _____

2. _____

3. _____

4. _____

5. _____

6. _____

FIRST LISTENING

CD 7, TR 3

Listen to the lecture on the U.S. Civil War. As you listen, put the following parts of the lecture in the order that you hear them. Number them 1 to 5.

_____ The attitude of Northerners and Southerners to slavery

_____ The strong economy of the northern states

_____ Lincoln's election as a cause of the civil war

_____ Statistics about how many people died during the U.S. Civil War

_____ The importance of slavery to southern agriculture

SECOND LISTENING

CD 7, TR 4

Listen to information from the lecture. The speaker will talk slowly and carefully. You don't have to do anything as you listen. Just relax and listen.

THIRD LISTENING

Listen to the lecture in two parts. Follow the directions for each part. When you have finished, review your notes. Later, you will use them to summarize the lecture with a partner.

Part 1

CD 7, TR 5

You will hear the first part of the lecture again. Listen and complete the notes by adding the abbreviations and symbols from the box.

CW   betw.   =   +   S.

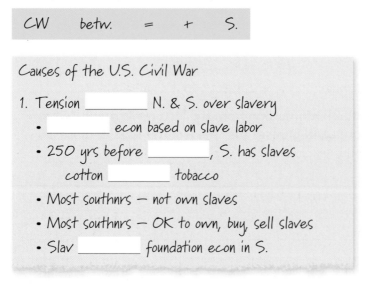

Causes of the U.S. Civil War

1. Tension _____ N. & S. over slavery

  • _____ econ based on slave labor

  • 250 yrs before _____, S. has slaves

    cotton _____ tobacco

  • Most southnrs — not own slaves

  • Most southnrs — OK to own, buy, sell slaves

  • Slav _____ foundation econ in S.

Part 2

CD 7, TR 5

As you listen to the second part of the lecture, take your own notes on a separate piece of paper.

ACCURACY CHECK

CD 7, TR 6

A You will hear four questions about the lecture. Write a short answer to each question. Use your notes.

1. _____
2. _____
3. _____
4. _____

CD 7, TR 6

B You will hear two sentences. One sentence mentions a cause and the other sentence gives the effect. You will be asked for either the *cause* or the *effect*. Write your answers below.

1. _____
2. _____
3. _____
4. _____
5. _____

ORAL SUMMARY

Use your notes to create an oral summary of the lecture with your partner. As you work together, add details to your notes that your partner included but you had missed.

DISCUSSION

Discuss the following questions with a classmate or in a small group.

1. Almost 200 movies have been made about the U.S. Civil War such as *Gone with the Wind* and *Gettysburg*. Can you name any others? Have you seen one? Or have you seen a movie about another civil war? How well did the movie show the causes and effects of the war?

2. You heard in the lecture that the U.S. Civil War is called other names such as the War between the States, the War of Rebellion, the War of Northern Aggression. Why do you think there are these different names and who do you think used them?

3. Discuss the causes and effects of one of the following: (1) an illness; (2) a trip to another country; (3) running a marathon; (4) winning an Olympic gold medal.

TASK 1 The Revolutionary War
CD 7, TR 7

Listen to sentences about the American Revolution. As you listen, complete the sentences by writing the missing words in the blanks.

1. The American Revolution started _____ the colonists wanted to have some form of _____.

2. The British were at a disadvantage during the war on _____ of the _____ that they were fighting a war far from their _____ country.

3. _____ the colonists had fewer weapons and _____ than the British, at times the colonists used some guerilla warfare _____.

4. One _____ that the colonists won the war was _____ the French entered the war on their _____.

TASK 2 Guessing Causes
CD 7, TR 8

Listen to each of the following situations. After you listen to each situation, quickly write down a possible cause or causes for the event you hear described.

1. Possible causes:

   _____

   _____

   _____

   _____

   _____

   _____

2. Possible causes:

   _____

   _____

   _____

   _____

   _____

   _____

3. Possible causes:

_____

_____

_____

_____

_____

_____

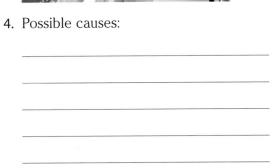

4. Possible causes:

_____

_____

_____

_____

_____

_____

5. Possible causes:

_____

_____

_____

_____

_____

_____

6. Possible causes:

_____

_____

_____

_____

_____

_____

CHAPTER 15

Endangered Species

Why Are They Endangered?

TOPIC PREVIEW

Answer the following questions with a partner or your classmates.

1. Think of an animal or plant species that is in danger of disappearing from the earth. Why is the animal or plant endangered?

2. What kinds of things do humans do that endanger species like the African elephant or rhinoceros? How do people help protect endangered species such as these animals?

3. How does air and water pollution endanger some species of fish, birds, and animals?

An endangered tortoise risks its life crossing the road in Wiggins, Mississippi.

VOCABULARY PREVIEW

 CD 7, TR 9

A **Listen to the following sentences that contain information from the lecture. As you listen, write the word or phrase from the box that completes the sentence.**

adapted	clear	dams	horns
introduced	related to	souvenirs	wildlife

1. Most animals and plants are _____ to live in a very specific environment.

2. Farmers _____ land to grow crops on.

3. We build _____ across rivers to produce electricity.

4. Closely _____ the destruction of habitats is the pollution of the environment.

5. Another major reason so many species are endangered is the illegal trade in

   _____ .

6. Elephant tusks are used to make _____ to sell to tourists.

7. Rhinoceroses, or rhinos, are killed for their _____ .

8. Some native species face competition from _____ species.

B **Match the words to their definitions.**

_____ 1. introduce

_____ 2. souvenir

_____ 3. wildlife

_____ 4. horn

_____ 5. clear

_____ 6. related to

_____ 7. dam

_____ 8. adapt

a. to put an animal or plant in a new region and environment

b. to become used to and depend on particular conditions

c. wild animals, birds, fish, etc., in their natural environment

d. a wall built to hold back water and make a lake

e. a hard pointed part growing from the head of some animals

f. something you buy or keep to remember a place you visited

g. to remove existing trees and other plants from an area of land

h. connected with another thing

PREDICTIONS

Think about the questions in the Topic Preview on page 112 and the sentences you heard in the Vocabulary Preview. Write three questions that you think will be answered in the lecture. Share your questions with your classmates.

NOTETAKING PREPARATION

Listening for a Review of the Lecture

Lecturers often repeat the main points of their lecture in their concluding remarks. Pay careful attention to this review at the end of a lecture and see if you have included the main points in your notes. If you find you have missed some important point, you can check after the lecture with your classmates or the lecturer to make your notes complete.

Listen for language such as the following to know that a review of the lecture is coming:

> *So, to review . . .*
> *So, to sum up . . .*
> *So, let me finish by going over the main points of today's lecture again.*
> *I'd like to finish by reviewing the main points of my lecture . . .*

A As you hear each statement, decide what the lecturer is next going to do: a, b, c, or d. Circle your choice.

CD 7, TR 10

a. preview the whole lecture	c. review the whole lecture
b. preview a main point in the lecture	d. review a main point in the lecture

1. a.   b.   c.   d.   4. a.   b.   c.   d.

2. a.   b.   c.   d.   5. a.   b.   c.   d.

3. a.   b.   c.   d.   6. a.   b.   c.   d.

Discourse Cues for Causal Analysis   Listen for the discourse cues that signal that a lecturer is discussing causes and effects. For a list of discourse cues for cause and effect, see page 100.

B Listen to sentences that contain information from the lecture. As you listen, write the missing words in the blanks to complete each sentence.

CD 7, TR 10

1. Most animals have disappeared from this planet _____ of natural _____ such as climate change.

2. Burning coal and oil can _____ acid rain, which results _____ a great deal of harm to an animal's habitat.

3. Competition for their habitat is a major _____ that animals are endangered. This is primarily a direct _____ of human activity.

4. Humans are also part of the natural world. _____, we need to protect plants and animals in order to protect our own future as a species.

FIRST LISTENING

CD 7, TR 11

Listen to the lecture on endangered species. As you listen, put the following parts of the lecture in the order that you hear them. Number them 1 to 5.

_____ Effects of rabbits introduced to Australia and brown tree snakes to Guam

_____ Different ways in which humans have destroyed animal habitats

_____ Reasons some animals are illegally hunted

_____ Human beings as a possible endangered species

_____ The effects of acid rain

SECOND LISTENING

CD 7, TR 12

Listen to information from the lecture. The speaker will talk slowly and carefully. You don't have to do anything as you listen. Just relax and listen.

THIRD LISTENING

Listen to the lecture in two parts. Follow the directions for each part. When you have finished, review your notes. Later, you will use them to summarize the lecture with a partner.

Part 1

CD 7, TR 13

You will hear the first part of the lecture again. Listen and complete the notes by adding the abbreviations and symbols from the box.

| hab | Poll. | nat | → | A. |

Reasons plants + anmls are end.
　　in past = _____ causes
　　today = hum act.
1. Destr. of + poll. of _____
　　Can't surv w/o spec hab, e.g., fish w/o water
　　_____ Destr. of hab
　　　　• e.g. clear forest
　　　　• empty wet areas
　　　　• build dams
　　　　All _____ destr of hab
　　B. _____ of env

Part 2

CD 7, TR 13

As you listen to the second part of the lecture, take your own notes on a separate piece of paper.

CD 7, TR 14

ACCURACY CHECK

You will hear 10 questions about the lecture. Write a short answer to each question. Use your notes.

1. _____
2. _____
3. _____
4. _____
5. _____
6. _____
7. _____
8. _____
9. _____
10. _____

ORAL SUMMARY

Use your notes to create an oral summary of the lecture with your partner. As you work together, add details to your notes that your partner included but you had missed.

DISCUSSION

Discuss the following questions with a classmate or in a small group.

1. What actions can you take personally to help safeguard an endangered species? Which one would you choose to help? How can you help?

2. Name two animals and plants that you think could be endangered 50 years from now by human activity or natural causes. Where do these animals and plants live and why would they become endangered?

3. What should be done to prevent the illegal hunting of elephants, rhinos, tigers, and other endangered species?

4. Do you believe zoos help save endangered species? What about circuses? What about research laboratories that, for example, experiment with monkeys and mice?

5. Do you believe it is as important to save an endangered butterfly as it is to save an endangered animal, such as the panda? Why or why not?

TASK 1 Endangered Species

CD 7, TR 15

A Listen to a short talk about endangered species. As you listen, fill in the missing information in the chart below.

Animal	Habitat	Reasons Endangered
Giant panda	China	1. Habitat destruction 2.
Blue whale		1. Killed for its meat 2.
California condor	Southern California, Arizona	1. 2. Killed to protect domestic animals
Snow leopard		1. Killed for fur 2.

CD 7, TR 15

B Listen to the questions. Write a short answer to each question you hear.

1. _____

2. _____

3. _____

4. _____

CD 7, TR 16

TASK 2 Types of Pollution

Listen to descriptions of the causes of five different types of pollution. As you listen, write the number of the description next to the type of pollution it causes.

_____ Noise pollution

_____ Light pollution

_____ Land pollution

_____ Air pollution

_____ Water pollution

The Surma People

TOPIC PREVIEW

Look at the photo and answer the following questions with a partner.

1. Where do you think the people in the photo live?

2. What do you think the reaction of these people was when two white middle-aged women arrived in their village?

3. Why do you think these women went to the village?

VOCABULARY PREVIEW

A **Read the definitions of these key words and phrases that you will hear during the video.**

remote far away from cities and towns

dense forest area of land thick with trees

bonded formed a close relationship

mule train a line of mules (horselike animals) used to carry things, often on land with no roads

ambushed attacked suddenly by people who were hiding

taken aback surprised; shocked

escort to go somewhere with someone, often to protect them

fingers crossed a gesture that you make when you want to be lucky and have no harm come to you

warriors fighters

B Work with a partner and write vocabulary from A in the blanks in the sentences.

1. The Surma people live in a _____ area, so the two women needed a _____ to help carry their supplies.

2. The women _____ with the Surma. They attended wedding and births. So, they were _____ when they learned some Surma wanted to kill them.

3. Some Surma _____ were chosen to _____ the women out of the _____ so that they would be able to leave safely.

4. The women had their _____, hoping they would not be _____ and killed.

🖥 FIRST VIEWING

Watch the video, and then compare your first impressions with a partner. Talk about what you remember, what surprised you, and what interested you.

🖥 SECOND VIEWING

Watch the video again. Listen for the missing words and write them in the blanks.

1. And our _____ was to find the Surma people, who live in the southwest, close to the _____ of Sudan.

2. We understood that our mule train was going to be ambushed, and that we would not be allowed out _____.

3. And what had happened is, unknowingly, we had broken a cardinal _____ of their society.

4. We would have a big _____ honoring the chiefs of the Surma.

5. So at 3:00 a.m., we packed up in the dark, put a chief in _____ each mule all the way down the line, and headed out in the pitch black of the _____ with our breath held and our fingers crossed.

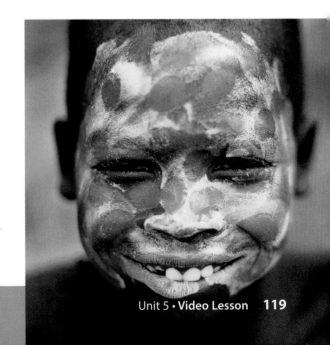

🖥 THIRD VIEWING

Complete these notes as you watch the video. Write only important words, not full sentences, and abbreviate common words.

1. The journey in

2. Bonding w/the Surma

3. The problem

4. The feast

5. The journey out

ORAL SUMMARY

Use your notes to create an oral summary of the video with your partner. As you work together, add details to your notes that your partner included but you had missed.

DISCUSSION

Discuss the following questions with a classmate or in a small group.

1. What were some causes and some effects in the story told by Carol Beckwith?

2. What does Carol Beckwith mean when she says, "We're here to tell the tale"?

3. Give an example of a situation where you had a cultural misunderstanding. What caused the misunderstanding?

Audioscripts

UNIT 1

Chronology

CHAPTER 1

Napoleon: From Schoolboy to Emperor

VOCABULARY PREVIEW Page 3

1. One of the most important historical figures in European history was Napoleon Bonaparte.
2. Napoleon excelled in mathematics and military science.
3. In 1785, Napoleon began the military career that brought him fame, power, riches, and finally, defeat.
4. Napoleon won many victories on the battlefield.
5. Napoleon became the first emperor of France.
6. At one time, Napoleon controlled most of Europe.
7. In his military campaign against Russia, Napoleon lost most of his army.
8. The great French conqueror died alone, deserted by his family and friends.

NOTETAKING PREPARATION Page 4

A

1. Napoleon was not a very good student.
2. Napoleon died alone in 1821 at the age of 51.
3. At school, Napoleon excelled at two subjects: math and military science.
4. At 16, he joined the French army.
5. He attacked Russia, but his army was defeated.

B

1. seventeen sixty-nine
2. seventeen eighty-five
3. eighteen O four
4. eighteen twenty-one

FIRST LISTENING Page 5

Lecturer: Today, I am going to talk to you about one of the most important historical figures in European history—Napoleon Bonaparte.

Let's start by talking about his early life. Napoleon was born in 1769 on the island of Corsica. When he was only 10 years old, his father sent him to military school in France. Napoleon was not a very good student in most of his classes, but he excelled in mathematics and in military science.

When Napoleon was 16 years old, he joined the French army. In that year, 1785, he began the military career that would bring him fame, power, riches, and, finally, defeat. After eight years in the army, Napoleon became a general. He was only 24. Napoleon had many victories on the battlefield, but he also became involved in French law and politics. And in 1804 at the age of 35, he became the first emperor of France.

Napoleon was many things. He was, first of all, a brilliant military leader. His soldiers were ready to die for him. As a result, Napoleon won many military victories. At one time he controlled most of Europe, but some countries, including England, Russia, and Austria, fought fiercely against Napoleon. His defeat—his end—came when he decided to attack Russia. In this military campaign against Russia, he lost most of his army.

The great French conqueror died alone, deserted by his family and his friends. The year was 1821, and Napoleon was only 51.

SECOND LISTENING Page 5

Napoleon was a French soldier. • Napoleon was born in 1769 on Corsica. • When he was 10, his father sent him to military school. • Napoleon was not a very good student. • He excelled in mathematics and in military science. • When he was 16, he joined the French army. • When he was 16, he began his military career. • His career brought him fame, power, riches, and finally, defeat. • Napoleon became a general when he was 24. • At the age of 35 he became emperor of France. • Napoleon was a great military leader. • His soldiers were ready to die for him. • Napoleon won many military victories. • At one time, he controlled most of Europe. • Some countries fought against him. • England, Russia, and Austria fought against him. • His defeat came when he attacked Russia. • During his fight with Russia, he lost most of his army. • Napoleon died alone in 1821. • He was deserted by his family and friends. • He was 51 years old when he died.

THIRD LISTENING Page 5

Part 1

Lecturer: Today, I am going to talk to you about one of the most important historical figures in European history—Napoleon Bonaparte.

Let's start by talking about his early life. Napoleon was born in 1769 on the island of Corsica. When he was only 10 years old, his father sent him to military school in France. Napoleon was not a very good student in most of his classes, but he excelled in mathematics and in military science.

When Napoleon was 16 years old, he joined the French army. In that year, 1785, he began the military career that would bring him fame, power, riches, and finally, defeat. After eight years in the army, Napoleon became a general. He was only 24.

Part 2

See First Listening, above.

ACCURACY CHECK Page 6

1. When was Napoleon born?
2. What kind of student was Napoleon in most of his classes?
3. What did Napoleon experience during his lifetime?
4. When did Napoleon become emperor of France?
5. One reason that Napoleon won many military victories was that his soldiers were ready to fight to the death for him.
6. Austria and Russia fought fiercely against Napoleon, but England did not.
7. Many of Napoleon's family and friends were with him when he died.
8. Napoleon died before he reached the age of 52.

EXPANSION TASK 1 Page 7

1. I was born around the year 1167 in Central Asia. I became the leader of my people and led my armies into many battles. I ruled one of the greatest empires the world has ever known. I am proud to say my name—Genghis Khan.
2. My name is Alexander the Great. I was born into a royal family and educated by the famous philosopher, Aristotle. In 334 BCE, I became the leader of my country at the age of 19. I was a great military leader, and at one time I controlled most of the known Western world.
3. I am Italian. I am Marco Polo. I traveled the Silk Road all the way to China in 1271. In China, I became a favorite of the ruler, Kublai Khan. Later I returned home to Venice where I dictated a book about my life and travels.
4. Some people know me as Suleiman the Magnificent. Some know me as the Lawgiver. When my father died in 1520, I became emperor of the large Ottoman Empire. But as a military leader of my people, I made my empire even bigger.
5. My name is Cleopatra. I was born into a royal family. I became queen at 18 and ruled Egypt for 21 years. The empire I created included most of the eastern Mediterranean coast. In 30 BCE, after I was defeated in battle, I committed suicide so that I could not be captured by my enemy, the Roman Emperor.
6. I am Attila, known as "Attila the Hun." I was born around 406. In the 440s, I conquered the eastern half of the Roman empire. In 450 I invaded Gaul, which is now France. My army was fierce and I was greatly feared by my enemies.

EXPANSION TASK 2 Page 8

The earliest "bicycle" appeared in France in the 1790s. It was a little wooden horse with a front wheel that could not be turned right or left. This little horse did not have any pedals, and the only way it could be moved was by the rider pushing against the ground with his or her feet.

In 1817, the German baron Karl von Drais made a front wheel that could turn. Now the rider could direct the wooden horse right or left. The rider still needed to push it with his or her feet on the ground.

The next development occurred in 1839, when a Scottish blacksmith, Kirkpatrick MacMillan, designed the first bicyclelike machine with pedals. MacMillan rode his machine the 70 miles from his home to Glasgow, Scotland, in only two days.

In 1866, Pierre Lallement applied for and received a U.S. patent for a machine that he called the "bisicle." Some people called it a "boneshaker" because it had steel wheels. Three years later, in 1869, rubber tires were introduced and the bicycle got more comfortable. Around the same time, the front wheels began to get larger and the back wheels got smaller. The first "highwheeler" was introduced in 1872. During the 1880s bicycles enjoyed a sudden growth in popularity. The highwheelers were very popular, especially among young men. They could go very fast, but they weren't very safe. A rider sitting high up on the bicycle and traveling very fast could easily fall off if the bicycle hit even a small bump in the road.

Fortunately, the "safety bicycle" was invented in 1884. The safety bicycle had equal-size wheels, a chain, and a gear-driven rear wheel. The rider was now sitting further back on the bicycle and in less danger. More improvements followed. Pneumatic tires—that is, tires with air in them—were invented in 1888. The last major innovation, the derailleur gear, arrived 11 years after that, in 1899.

Beginning in the 1970s, bicycles became lighter, and changes in design and materials allowed bicycles to go faster. No doubt there will be more improvements in design and materials in the future.

CHAPTER 2

Pompeii: Destroyed, Forgotten, and Found

VOCABULARY PREVIEW Page 10

1. Many rich people who live in large metropolitan areas leave the city in the summer and go to the mountains or to the seashore.
2. In the summer of the year 79 CE, a young Roman boy was visiting his uncle at Pompeii.
3. Pliny saw the eruption of the volcano called Mount Vesuvius.
4. Rock and ash flew through the air.
5. When the eruption was over, Pompeii was buried under 20 feet of volcanic rock and ash.
6. In 1748, an Italian farmer digging on his farm uncovered part of a wall of the ancient city of Pompeii.
7. Soon, archaeologists began to dig in the area.
8. Today, tourists come from all over the world to see the ruins of the famous city of Pompeii.

NOTETAKING PREPARATION Page 11

1. A boy looked up in the sky.
2. The boy later became a famous Roman historian.
3. There was no time to escape. As a result many were buried alive.
4. More than 2,000 people died.
5. Pompeii was forgotten for almost 1,700 years.

1. Today, many rich people leave the city for the summer.
2. Two thousand years ago, rich people did the same thing.
3. In the year 79 CE, a young boy was visiting his uncle.
4. The city was forgotten for almost 1,700 years.
5. As time went by, much of the ancient city was uncovered.

FIRST LISTENING Page 12

Lecturer: The lecture for this class is about the city of Pompeii and the natural disaster that occurred there almost 2,000 years ago.

Today, many rich people who live in large metropolitan areas such as Beijing, Paris, and New York leave the city in the summer. They go to the mountains or to the seashore to escape the city noise and heat. Two thousand years ago, wealthy Romans did the same thing. They left the city of Rome in the summer. Many of these wealthy Romans spent their summers in the city of Pompeii, a beautiful city located on the Bay of Naples, on the Mediterranean Sea.

In the summer of the year 79 CE, a young Roman boy who later became a very famous Roman historian was visiting his uncle in Pompeii. The boy's name was Pliny the Younger. One day Pliny was looking up at the sky. He saw a frightening sight. It was a very large dark cloud. This black cloud rose high into the sky. What Pliny saw was the eruption of the volcano called Mount Vesuvius. Rock and ash flew through the air. The city of Pompeii was at the foot of Mount Vesuvius.

When the volcano first erupted, many people were able to get out of the city and escape death. In fact, 18,000 people escaped the terrible disaster. Unfortunately, there was not enough time for everyone to escape. More than 2,000 people died. These unlucky people were buried alive under the volcanic ash. The eruption lasted for about three days. When the eruption was over, Pompeii was buried under 20 feet of volcanic rock and ash. The city of Pompeii was forgotten for almost 1,700 years.

In the year 1748 an Italian farmer was digging on his farm. As he was digging, he uncovered a part of a wall of the ancient city of Pompeii. Soon, archaeologists began to dig in the area. As time went by, much of the ancient city of Pompeii was uncovered. Today, tourists come from all over the world to see the ruins of the famous city of Pompeii.

SECOND LISTENING Page 12

Two thousand years ago, many Romans left Rome in the summer. • Many of these wealthy Romans spent their summer in Pompeii. • Pompeii was located on the Bay of Naples. • In 79 CE, a young Roman boy was visiting his uncle in Pompeii. • One day Pliny saw a frightening sight. • He saw a very large dark cloud. • This cloud rose high into the sky. • Pliny saw the eruption of Vesuvius. • Pompeii was at the foot of Mount Vesuvius. • Many people were able to flee the city. • Eighteen thousand people escaped death. • More than 2,000 people died. • They were buried alive under the volcanic ash. • The eruption lasted for about three days. • Pompeii was buried under 20 feet of volcanic rock and ash. • Pompeii was forgotten for 1,700 years. • In 1748 an Italian farmer uncovered a part of Pompeii. • Archaeologists began to dig in the area. • As time went by, much of the ancient city of Pompeii was uncovered. • Today tourists come from all over the world to see the ruins of Pompeii.

THIRD LISTENING Page 12

Part 1

Lecturer: The lecture for this class is about the city of Pompeii and the natural disaster that occurred there almost 2,000 years ago.

Today many rich people who live in large metropolitan areas such as Beijing, Paris, and New York leave the city in the summer. They go to the mountains or to the seashore to escape the city noise and heat. Two thousand years ago, wealthy Romans did the same thing. They left the city of Rome in the summer. Many of these wealthy Romans spent their summers in the city of Pompeii, a beautiful city located on the Bay of Naples, on the Mediterranean Sea.

In the summer of the year 79 CE, a young Roman boy who later became a very famous Roman historian was visiting his uncle in Pompeii. The boy's name was Pliny the Younger.

Part 2

See First Listening, above.

ACCURACY CHECK Page 13

1. At what time of year did wealthy Romans like to visit Pompeii?
2. In what year did Pliny visit his uncle in Pompeii?
3. What did Pliny see when he looked up in the sky?
4. In what year did an Italian farmer discover part of a wall of Pompeii?
5. Most of the people in Pompeii were able to leave the city and escape death.
6. Rome was located at the foot of Mount Vesuvius.
7. The Italian farmer was looking for the ancient city of Pompeii.
8. Pompeii was buried and forgotten between 79 and 1748 CE.

EXPANSION TASK 1 Page 14

1. Marco took his exam on Friday. He received his test results in the mail four days later on Tuesday.
2. Sixty years ago, nobody had personal computers in their homes. Today, almost every home in the United States has at least one and often more than one computer.

3. The volcano erupted violently and ash came down covering the city. For three days before that, there had been several small earthquakes shaking the city.
4. The Summer Olympics in 2004 were held in the Greek capital, Athens. The first modern Olympic Games were also held in Athens more than 100 years earlier in 1896.
5. Four days ago, Jackie started a new job as a sales manager for a big company. This was just four weeks after she lost her job as an assistant sales manager for a small company.
6. In 1271, Marco Polo left Venice with his father on a long journey across land to China. He returned 24 years later in 1295 as a rich man.

See A, above.

EXPANSION TASK 2 Page 15

The eruption of Mount Vesuvius was probably the most famous volcanic eruption in history. Mount Vesuvius is located in Italy. In 79 CE, the volcano erupted, shooting a giant cloud of ash into the air, which buried the city of Pompeii. Approximately 2,000 people died in the eruption. Let's compare Mount Vesuvius with some other famous volcanic eruptions.

Cotopaxi is a volcano located in Ecuador. It erupted in 1877, and about 1,000 people died.

Krakatoa was another large volcano. It erupted in 1883 in Indonesia. The volcano erupted in a giant explosion, which killed about 36,000 people.

The small country of Martinique is home to the volcano called Mont Pelée. It erupted in 1902, killing approximately 38,000 people.

Mount St. Helens is a volcano located in the state of Washington in the United States. It erupted in 1980 and destroyed the entire side of the mountain. Luckily, only 57 people were killed.

The eruption of Mount Tambora in 1815 was the most deadly volcanic eruption in history. When Mount Tambora erupted in Indonesia, about 71,000 people died.

CHAPTER 3

Steve Jobs: A Man with a Vision

VOCABULARY PREVIEW Page 17

1. Jobs' friend Stephen Wozniak liked to design and build his own electronic equipment.

2. Jobs and Wozniak founded the Apple Computer company.

3. The Apple II became the world's first mass-produced personal computer.

4. The movie *Toy Story* was the first full-length, computer-generated, animated film.

5. Pixar became a very, very profitable company.

6. In 2001 Jobs introduced Apple's "digital hub" strategy.

7. The iPhone was like having an iPod, a camera, and a phone all in one device.

8. Three years later, Jobs released the iPad onto the market.

NOTETAKING PREPARATION   Page 18

In 1998, Apple introduced the iMac, a new desktop computer. And the following year, they brought out the iBook, a new laptop computer. A couple of years later, in 2001, the company introduced the iPod, which quickly became the most popular digital music player. And in January 2007, Apple introduced the iPhone, which was like having, not only a phone, but a mini computer in your hand.

1. The next year Jobs and Wozniak founded the Apple Computer company.

2. By the age of 25, Steve Jobs was a millionaire.

3. In 1995, Pixar released the movie *Toy Story*.

4. Over the next 10 years, Apple introduced many new products.

5. Three years later, Jobs released the iPad onto the market.

FIRST LISTENING   Page 19

Lecturer: I'd like to talk to you today about Steve Jobs. Jobs was someone who changed the world, because he changed the way people act every single day.

Jobs was born in 1955. He grew up in California, in an area that later became known as the Silicon Valley. When he was about 14 years old, he became friends with Stephen Wozniak. Wozniak was what people in those days called an electronics "whiz kid." He liked to design and build his own electronic equipment.

In 1975, Wozniak started designing a personal computer. This was at a time when nobody owned personal computers in their homes. Jobs was young. He was only 20. But even then he had a sharp business brain. Jobs convinced Wozniak that they could build these personal computers in his garage and sell them. A year later, Jobs and Wozniak founded the Apple

Computer company, and started building and selling personal computers.

When their Apple II computer went on the market in 1977, it became a huge success! Suddenly, there was a mass market for a computer that people could buy at a store and use sitting in their own homes! The Apple II became the world's first mass-produced personal computer, and by the age of 25, Steve Jobs was a millionaire.

Jobs was brilliant in many ways, but he was not always very good at working with other people. He needed everything to be perfect, and this caused problems at Apple. In 1985, then, Jobs left Apple and started a new computer company, and soon after he also went into business with a company called Pixar. Pixar was a company trying to develop a system for using CGI—computer-generated imagery—to be used in animated films. And Jobs was just the person to help them.

In 1995, Pixar released the movie *Toy Story*. It was the first full-length, computer-generated, animated film. It was a big hit and Pixar became a very, very profitable company and Steve Jobs became a very, very rich man—a billionaire in fact.

In the 10 years after leaving Apple, Jobs learned a lot about working with people and running a company. So when he returned to Apple in 1995, he made many changes.

Without Jobs, Apple was not doing so well. But Jobs had a vision. He didn't only want personal computers to be useful, he also wanted them to be beautiful objects that people would enjoy looking at and using. In 1998, Apple introduced the iMac, a new desktop computer, and the next year, the iBook, a new laptop computer. People thought both were very attractive and they immediately became very popular, and Apple became a profitable company again.

But Steve Jobs wasn't finished. He had an even bigger vision. He believed that personal computers would become the center, *the hub*, of people's digital lives. So in 2001 Jobs introduced Apple's "digital hub" strategy. He told the world that the computer would become the hub of all their electronic equipment. You could connect your camera, your music player, and your video recorder to the computer and manage all your videos, photos, and music using iTunes, iMovie, iPhoto, and other Apple programs, or "apps." Over the next 10 years, Apple created products that made Jobs' vision a reality. In 2001, the company introduced the iPod, which quickly became the most popular digital music player. In January 2007, Jobs introduced the iPhone and suddenly your phone became like a mini computer. It was like having an iPod, a camera, and a phone all in one device that you could hold in your hand. Then three years later he released the iPad onto the market. This really was a small, light computer that you could hold in your hand. And to use it all you had to do was touch the screen.

Jobs' final vision before he died in October 2011 was Apple iCloud. This is a system that allows Apple users to store and manage their data and applications, not in their computer, but over the Internet.

Jobs may be gone, but there is no question that his vision lives on. Jobs was someone who changed the world, not just for our own time, but maybe, who knows, for all time.

SECOND LISTENING Page 19

Jobs was someone who changed the world. • He changed the way people act every single day. • Jobs was born in 1955. • He grew up in California, in Silicon Valley. • When he was about 14 years old, he became friends with Stephen Wozniak. • Wozniak was an electronics "whiz kid." • He liked to design and build electronic equipment. • In 1975, Wozniak started designing a personal computer. • Nobody owned personal computers in their homes. • Jobs was young. • He was only 20. • But even then he had a sharp business brain. • Jobs and Wozniak built personal computers in a garage to sell. • A year later, Jobs and Wozniak founded the Apple Computer company. • The Apple II computer went on the market in 1977. • The Apple II became the world's first mass-produced personal computer. • By the age of 25, Steve Jobs was a millionaire. • Jobs was not always very good at working with other people. • He needed everything to be perfect, and this caused problems. • In 1985, Jobs left Apple. • Soon after he went into business with Pixar. • Pixar was a company that developed computer-generated imagery. • CGI was to be used in animated films. • In 1995, Pixar released the movie *Toy Story*. • It was the first full-length, computer-generated, animated film. • Pixar became a very, very profitable company. • Steve Jobs became a billionaire. • Ten years after leaving Apple, Jobs returned in 1995. • Without Jobs, Apple was not doing so well. • Jobs had a vision. • He wanted personal computers to be useful and beautiful objects. • In 1998, Apple introduced a new desktop computer, the iMac. • The next year, Apple introduced a new laptop computer, the iBook. • The iMac and the iBook immediately became very popular. • Apple became a profitable company again. • Jobs had a bigger vision. • He believed personal computers would become *the hub* of people's lifestyles. • In 2001, Jobs introduced Apple's "digital hub" strategy. • The computer would become the hub of all their electronic equipment. • You could connect your camera, music player, and video recorder to the computer. • You could manage your videos, photos, and music using iTunes, iMovie, and iPhoto. • You could use other Apple programs, or "apps." • Over the next 10 years, Apple

created products that made Jobs' vision a reality. • In 2001, the company introduced the iPod. • It quickly became the most popular digital music player. • In January 2007, Jobs introduced the iPhone. • Suddenly your phone became like a mini computer. • It was like having an iPod, a camera, and a phone in one device. • You could hold the iPhone in your hand. • Three years later he released the iPad onto the market. • The iPad was a small, light computer you could hold in your hand. • To use it all you had to do was touch the screen. • Jobs' final vision before he died in October 2011 was Apple iCloud. • It allows Apple users to store and manage data and applications over the Internet. • Jobs may be gone, but there is no question his vision lives on. • Jobs changed the world, not just for our time. • Jobs maybe changed the world for all time.

THIRD LISTENING Page 19

Part 1

Lecturer: I'd like to talk to you today about Steve Jobs. Jobs was someone who changed the world, because he changed the way people act every single day.

Jobs was born in 1955. He grew up in California, in an area that later became known as the Silicon Valley. When he was about 14 years old, he became friends with Stephen Wozniak. Wozniak was what people in those days called an electronics "whiz kid." He liked to design and build his own electronic equipment.

In 1975, Wozniak started designing a personal computer. This was at a time when nobody owned personal computers in their homes. Jobs was young. He was only 20. But even then he had a sharp business brain. Jobs convinced Wozniak that they could build these personal computers in his garage and sell them. A year later, Jobs and Wozniak founded the Apple Computer company, and started building and selling personal computers.

When their Apple II computer went on the market in 1977, it became a huge success! Suddenly, there was a mass market for a computer that people could buy at a store and use sitting in their own homes! The Apple II became the world's first mass-produced personal computer, and by the age of 25, Steve Jobs was a millionaire.

Part 2

See First Listening, above.

ACCURACY CHECK Page 20

1. When was Steve Jobs born?
2. How old was Steve Jobs when he met a new friend named Steve Wozniak?

3. At what age did Steve Jobs become a millionaire?

4. In what year did Jobs return to lead the Apple company after he had left it?

5. When did the iMac make an appearance on the market?

6. In what year did Steve Jobs die?

1. Where did Steve Jobs grow up?

2. Who was Steve Wozniak?

3. What did Steve Jobs do for the 10 years after he had left Apple in 1985?

4. What was the last product Steve Jobs introduced to the world?

EXPANSION TASK 1 Page 21

Was a computer always a computer? What we think of as a computer started out as a device known as an "abacus." The abacus was invented in Babylonia around 300 BCE. For hundreds of years, the abacus was the main tool for counting. Much later, in 1642, Blaise Pascal invented the first true calculator. It did not run on electricity. It could add numbers by turning gears. About 30 years later, in 1673, Gottfried Wilhelm Leibniz created a calculator that could add, subtract, multiply, and divide. It also used gears and wheels.

More than a hundred years passed. Then, in 1801, Joseph-Marie Jacquard invented a punch card for weaving cloth. The holes in the cards created a code that made sure that the threads went through in the right order. This system of codes would eventually be used in modern computers. Not many years later, in 1833, Charles Babbage began designing a very basic computer that would use punch cards. Babbage thought of many of the parts of the modern computer and today he is known as the "father of the computer." In the late 1880s Herman Hollerith invented a calculating machine that counted and sorted information with punch cards.

A critical moment was now coming up. In the 1940s computers were huge machines that used vacuum tubes. From this point on, computer technology grew very quickly. Throughout the 1950s computers became faster and ran on silicon chips. In the 1960s, computers became more affordable and small enough to fit in a home. The 1980s saw the beginning of the computers like those we use today. Since the 1980s computers have become even faster, smaller, and more powerful, and today they are an important part of our world.

EXPANSION TASK 2 Page 21

1. Mark Zuckerberg started the social media site Facebook when he was only 20 years old. It was one of the first social media Internet sites, and its popularity grew very quickly. In 2008, when Mark Zuckerberg was 24 years old, the Facebook Web site had reached 100 million total users.

2. Jimmy Wales had an idea for an online encyclopedia that anyone could add information to. He started a Web site called Wikipedia on January 15, 2001. Two years later, Wikipedia had 100,000 articles on the Web site. Seven years after that, Wikipedia had over 3 million articles in English on their Web site.

3. Amazon.com was one of the first Web sites where people could buy products online. It was started in the United States in 1995 by Jeff Bezos. When it began, it was an online bookstore. In its first five years, Amazon.com did not make any profit. Today, however, Amazon.com is one of the biggest online shopping Web sites in the world.

4. Larry Page and Sergey Brin created a company called Google. Today, Google.com is the most popular Web site in the world, and has over 600 million visitors every day. But Google is more than just one Web site. Eight years after Larry Page started Google, it purchased the Web site YouTube.com. One year later, in 2007, Google started creating mobile phones.

5. Bill Gates was born in 1955. Twenty years later, Gates left college to start a company called Microsoft. In 1983, Bill Gates and his company announced a program for computers called Microsoft Windows. Windows quickly became used in computers all over the world, and Bill Gates became extremely wealthy. Thirty-five years after he started his company, Bill Gates was worth 53 billion dollars!

6. Twitter is a popular social media Web site where people can send and read messages. In 2012 Twitter had over 500 million users all over the world. Only six years before that, Jack Dorsey created the Web site in San Francisco.

See A, above.

UNIT 2

Process

CHAPTER 4

Roller Coasters: The Ups and Downs of How They Work

VOCABULARY PREVIEW   Page 27

1. Let's talk about the physics involved in a ride on a roller coaster.

2. A simple roller coaster consists of a frame with a track on it.

3. The track follows a path that ends at the same place it started.

4. The roller-coaster cars have two sets of wheels.

5. The wheels below the track keep the fast-moving cars from coming off the track.

6. At the top of the first hill, the chain comes off the cars and gravity takes over.

7. The cars gain speed as they roll downhill.

8. Then they go down a very steep slope.

9. The cars travel in a loop that puts us upside down.

NOTETAKING PREPARATION   Page 28

This is basically how roller coasters work. First, a chain pulls a roller-coaster car uphill. At the top of the hill, the chain comes off and gravity then pushes the car downhill very fast. At the bottom of the hill, the car now has enough energy to go up the next hill.

C

1. A chain pulls the car up the first hill, but then comes off at the top.

2. At this point, there is enough energy to push the cars up the next hill.

3. The cars begin to slow down during this stage.

4. Finally, the cars roll to a stop.

FIRST LISTENING   Page 29

Lecturer: Let's talk a little today about how roller coasters work and the physics involved in a ride on a roller coaster. I'm sure many of you have taken a ride on a roller coaster. Personally, I don't ever want to ride on one again. When I was young, my sister took me on a roller coaster, and I never forgot that frightening experience.

A simple roller coaster consists of a frame with a track on it. The track is very much like a train track. This track goes over a series of hills and around curves following a path that ends at the same place it started. A train of cars travels around on this track, very fast. The cars have two sets of wheels. One set of wheels rolls on top of the track and the other set of wheels rolls below the track. The wheels below the track are there to keep the fast-moving cars from coming off the track.

Roller-coaster cars, as you probably know, don't have any motors or engines. Instead, a chain pulls the cars up the first, tallest and steepest, hill. And this is how the ride begins. Then, at the top of the hill, the chain comes off the cars, and gravity takes over. Gravity pushes the cars down the other side of the hill. The taller and steeper the first hill is, the faster the ride will be, and the farther the cars will travel.

As the cars roll downhill, they gain speed. When they reach the bottom of the first hill, the cars have enough speed and energy to send them up the next hill. As the cars near the top of the second hill, they begin to slow down. But then, the cars reach the top of that hill and start down the other side, and gravity again pushes them toward the ground. This process repeats on each hill.

OK, so let's go over this process again. First, the cars are pulled by a chain up the first, highest hill. Then they go down a very steep slope. At this point, there is enough energy to pull the cars up and over the next hill. Again, when they reach the bottom of that hill, there is enough energy to climb the next hill. The roller-coaster cars lose energy as the ride continues, so the hills have to be smaller toward the end of the track. Finally, we roll to a stop on ground level, right where we began.

Tomorrow we will talk about the forces that press on our bodies and keep us in our seats when the cars of a roller coaster travel in a loop that puts us upside down.

SECOND LISTENING   Page 29

Let's talk about the physics involved in a ride on a roller coaster. • I'm sure many of you have taken a ride on a roller coaster. • A simple roller coaster consists of a frame with a track on it. • The track is very much like a train track. • This track goes over a series of hills and around curves. • It follows a path that ends at the same place it started. • A train of cars travels around on this track, very fast. • The cars have two sets of wheels. • One set of wheels rolls on top of the track, and the other set of wheels rolls below the track. • The wheels below the track keep the fast-moving cars from coming off the track. • Roller-coaster cars, as you probably know, don't have any motors or engines. • Instead, a chain pulls the cars up the first, tallest and steepest, hill. • This is how the ride begins. • Then, at the top of the hill the chain comes off the cars and gravity takes over. • Gravity pushes the cars down the other side of the hill. • The taller and steeper the first hill is, the faster the ride will be. • And the farther the cars will travel. • As the cars roll downhill, they gain speed. • The cars have enough speed and energy to send them up the next hill. • As the cars near the top of the second hill, they begin to slow down. • But then, the cars reach the top of that hill and start down the other side. • Gravity again pushes them toward the ground. • This process repeats on each hill. • OK, so let's go over this process again. • First, the cars are pulled by a chain up the first, highest hill. • Then they go down a very steep slope. • At this point, there is enough energy to pull the cars up and over the next hill. • When they reach the bottom of that hill, there is enough energy to climb the next hill. • The roller-coaster cars lose energy as the ride continues. • So, the hills have to be smaller toward the end of the track. • Finally, we roll to a stop on ground level, right where we began.

THIRD LISTENING Page 29

Part 1

Lecturer: Let's talk a little today about how roller coasters work and the physics involved in a ride on a roller coaster. I'm sure many of you have taken a ride on a roller coaster. Personally, I don't ever want to ride on one again. When I was young, my sister took me on a roller coaster, and I never forgot that frightening experience.

A simple roller coaster consists of a frame with a track on it. The track is very much like a train track. This track goes over a series of hills and around curves following a path that ends at the same place it started. A train of cars travels around on this track, very fast. The cars have two sets of wheels. One set of wheels rolls on top of the track and the other set of wheels rolls below the track. The wheels below the track are there to keep the fast-moving cars from coming off the track.

Part 2

See First Listening, above.

ACCURACY CHECK Page 30

1. What does a simple roller coaster consist of?
2. What was the roller coaster compared to in the lecture?
3. What pulls the roller coaster up the first steep hill?
4. What pushes the roller coaster down the hills?
5. What area of science did the speaker refer to in the lecture?
6. What happens near the end of the roller-coaster ride?

1. How do the two sets of wheels function on the roller-coaster car?
2. When does the chain that pulls the roller coaster up the first hill come off?
3. When does gravity function in the roller-coaster ride?
4. What happens when the roller coaster nears the end of the ride?
5. What puts people upside down on a roller-coaster ride?

EXPANSION TASK 1 Page 31

Taking your pulse is easy. Just follow these steps.

First, have a watch with a second hand ready or use the stopwatch on your cell phone.

To start with, put the middle three fingers of your right hand on your left wrist just below your thumb. Press down a little until you feel your pulse beat. Can you feel your pulse?

Look at the second hand on your watch and start counting the beats that you are feeling with your fingers. After 30 seconds, stop counting and write down the number of beats that you felt in 30 seconds.

Wait a few seconds and then repeat the process. Write down the second number and add it to the first number. This is your pulse rate.

EXPANSION TASK 2 Page 32

Pose 1. First, lie on your stomach with your legs together. The legs should be straight out behind you. Now put your hands under your shoulders. Slowly raise yourself up. Make your arms straight and bend your back up as far as it can go.

Pose 2. To get into this position, first lie on your back. Put your hands on your back. Now slowly bend your knees and raise your back until your knees are pointing at your chin. Slowly bring your legs up straight so that your toes are now pointing up in the air.

Pose 3. To get into this position, follow the directions for pose two. Then slowly lower your legs behind you so that you are looking up at your knees. If you can, touch the ground with your toes. Take your hands off your back and lay them down straight behind you.

Pose 4. Stand up straight looking straight ahead. Raise both arms slowly above your head and bring your hands together. Now slowly raise your right leg up so that your right foot is touching your left knee. Hold that position for a few seconds.

Pose 5. Sit on your knees with your body straight up. Face forward. Raise both arms up in the air above your head. Now slowly bend your body forward. Keep your arms straight and let them touch the ground in front of you. If you can, try to touch the ground in front of you with your forehead.

Pose 6. Start at the position as in pose 5. From this position, slowly straighten your legs and bring your bottom up off the ground. When you are in the final position, your hands will be on the ground in front of you and your arms will be straight. Your legs will also be straight.

First, stand up straight and look straight ahead. Next, raise both arms slowly above your head. Now bring your hands together until they are touching. The next step is to slowly raise your right leg up so that your right foot is touching your left knee. Now hold that position for a few seconds.

CHAPTER 5

Language: How Children Acquire Theirs

VOCABULARY PREVIEW Page 34

1. A few weeks after birth, babies start to make cooing noises when they're happy.
2. Around four months of age, babies begin to babble.
3. By 10 months old, the babbling of babies from different language backgrounds sounds different.
4. At first, babies invent their own words for things.
5. In the next few months, babies will acquire a lot of words.
6. These words are usually the names of things that are in the baby's environment.
7. The speech young children produce is often called "telegraphic" speech because they leave out all but the most essential words.
8. Babies begin to overgeneralize a grammar rule and make a lot of grammar mistakes.

NOTETAKING PREPARATION Page 35

1. Babies all over the world begin to babble around the same age.
2. The next stage of language acquisition begins around 18 months.
3. In the next few months, babies will acquire a lot of words.

4. In other words, they learn the rule for making the past tense of many verbs.
5. Think about how the process of learning a first and second language may be similar and different.

What I'd like to talk to you about today is child language development. I know that you all are trying to learn a second language, but for a moment, let's think about a related topic: How children learn their first language. What do we know about how babies develop their language and communication ability?

FIRST LISTENING Page 36

Lecturer: What I'd like to talk to you about today is child language development. I know that you all are trying to learn a second language, but for a moment, let's think about a related topic: How children learn their first language. What do we know about how babies develop their language and communication ability? Well, we know babies are able to communicate as soon as they are born—even before they learn to speak. At first, they communicate by crying. This crying lets their parents know when they are hungry, or unhappy, or uncomfortable. However, they soon begin the process of acquiring language. The first stage begins a few weeks after birth. At this stage, babies start to make cooing noises when they are happy. Then, at around four months they begin to babble. Babies all over the world begin to babble around the same age, and they all begin to make the same kinds of babbling noises. By the time they are ten months old, however, the babbling of babies from different language backgrounds sounds different. For example, the babbling of a baby in a Chinese-speaking home sounds different from the babbling of a baby in an English-speaking home.

Babies begin a new stage of language development when they start to speak their first words. At first, they invent their own words for things. For example, a baby in an English-speaking home may say "baba" for the word *ball* or "kiki" for *cat*. In the next few months, babies will acquire a lot of words. These words are usually the names of things that are in the baby's environment, words for food or toys, for example. They will begin to use these words to communicate with others. For example, if a baby holds up an empty juice cup and says "juice," the baby seems to be saying, "I want more juice" or "May I have more juice?" This word *juice* is really a one-word sentence.

The next stage of language acquisition begins around 18 months, when babies begin to say two-word sentences. They use a kind of grammar to put words together. The babies produce what is called "telegraphic" speech, meaning they leave out all but the most essential words. An English-speaking child might say something like "Daddy, up," which actually means "Daddy, pick me up, please." Then, between two and three years of age, children learn more and more grammar. For example, they begin to use the past tense of verbs. In other words, they learn the rule for making the past tense of many verbs. The children begin to say things such as "I walked home" and "I kissed Mommy." They also overgeneralize this new grammar rule and make a lot of mistakes. For example, children often say such things as "I goed to bed" instead of "I went to bed," or "I eated ice cream" instead of "I ate ice cream." In other words, the children have learned the past-tense rule for regular verbs such as *walk* and *kiss*, but they haven't learned that they cannot use this rule for all verbs. Some verbs like *eat* are irregular, and the past tense forms for irregular verbs must be learned individually. Anyway, these mistakes are normal. The children will soon learn to use the past tense for regular and irregular verbs correctly. They then continue to learn other grammatical structures in the same way.

If we stop to think about it, it's quite amazing how quickly children all over the world learn their language. It's also amazing how similar the process is for babies all over the world.

You probably don't remember anything about how you learned your first language. But now that you've learned something about the process, think about how the process of learning a first and second language may be similar and different. After class, why not make a list of some similarities and differences in the processes of child and adult language learning. Then we'll talk about it next time we meet.

SECOND LISTENING Page 36

Today I'd like to talk about the topic of child language development. • How do children learn their first language? • What do we know about how babies develop their language and communication ability? • We know babies are able to communicate as soon as they are born. • Babies are able to communicate even before they learn to speak. • At first, they communicate by crying. • This crying lets their parents know how they feel. • Their parents know if they are hungry, or unhappy, or uncomfortable. • Babies soon begin to acquire language. • The first stage begins a few weeks after birth. • Babies start to make cooing noises. • At around four months babies begin to babble. • All babies begin to babble at the same age. • All babies make the same babbling noises. • By ten months the babbling of babies sounds different. • At this time a new stage of language learning begins. • Now babies begin to make their first words. • They invent their own words. • These words are the babies' own words for things, like "kiki"

for *cat*. • Soon after, babies begin to learn the names of many things. • These are things in their environment. • They learn the words for toys and food, for example. • They begin to use these words to communicate. • They begin to make one-word sentences. • For example, they hold up their cup and say "juice." • The next stage begins at about 18 months of age. • At 18 months they begin to make two-word sentences. • They use a kind of grammar to put these two words together. • This language is called "telegraphic" speech. • Telegraphic language has only the most essential words. • Between two and three years of age children learn more grammar rules. • For example, they begin to use the past tense rule for regular verbs. • They overgeneralize the past tense rule to irregular verbs. • They make lots of mistakes. • For example, they say "I goed to bed" instead of "I went to bed." • Their mistakes are natural at this age. • They continue to learn more grammatical structures in the same way. • This process is similar for babies all over the world. • You probably don't remember how you learned your first language. • Think about how the process of learning a first and second language is similar or different. • Make a list of the similarities and differences. • We'll talk about it next time.

THIRD LISTENING Page 36

Part 1

Lecturer: What I'd like to talk to you about today is child language development. I know that you all are trying to learn a second language, but for a moment, let's think about a related topic: How children learn their first language. What do we know about how babies develop their language and communication ability? Well, we know babies are able to communicate as soon as they are born—even before they learn to speak. At first, they communicate by crying. This crying lets their parents know when they are hungry, or unhappy, or uncomfortable. However, they soon begin the process of acquiring language. The first stage begins a few weeks after birth.

At this stage, babies start to make cooing noises when they are happy. Then, at around four months they begin to babble. Babies all over the world begin to babble around the same age, and they all begin to make the same kinds of babbling noises. By the time they are ten months old, however, the babbling of babies from different language backgrounds sounds different. For example, the babbling of a baby in a Chinese-speaking home sounds different from the babbling of a baby in an English-speaking home.

Babies begin a new stage of language development when they start to speak their first words.

Part 2

See First Listening, above.

ACCURACY CHECK Page 37

1. At what age do babies begin to communicate?

2. Which of the following is an example of "telegraphic" speech?

3. At what age do children begin to use the past tense?

4. At four months of age, the babbling of babies sounds the same all over the world.

5. A baby's first words are usually words that he or she invents.

6. A child uses only vocabulary and no grammar before about two years of age.

7. Children probably say "I goed" instead of "I went" because they hear their parents say this.

EXPANSION TASK 1 Page 38

1. Milk.

2. I goed park and played.

3. No bed.

4. Goo ga goo ga goo.

5. Me want doggie, Mommy.

C

See A, above.

EXPANSION TASK 2 Page 38

A

1. Write a clear subject in the subject box.

2. Keep your e-mail message brief.

3. Express yourself clearly and politely.

4. Check your spelling and grammar.

5. Read your e-mail before sending it.

CHAPTER 6

Robots: How They Work and Learn to Work

VOCABULARY PREVIEW Page 40

A

1. Today, I'm going to talk mostly about industrial robots.

2. These robots do work that is repetitive, dangerous, or boring.

3. The robot learns to do its job with the guidance of a human being.

4. Robotic arms on the assembly line join the parts of a car together.

5. Robots are very precise when repeating a task.

6. Robots do work humans could do, but they do it more efficiently.

7. The robot stores the exact movements in its computer memory.

8. A robot uses sensors to gather information.

9. An autonomous machine can change its behavior in relation to its surroundings.

10. Honda's ASIMO can detect the movements of people nearby.

NOTETAKING PREPARATION Page 41

1. When people think about a robot, they often picture a machine that looks something like a human being.

2. So, just how do robots work?

3. The robots we are going to talk about now are known as "autonomous" robots.

See A, above.

1. First, a person must use a handheld computer.

2. So now, the robot will use its sensors to direct its actions.

3. The robot "tells" its moving parts what to do and then it performs the action.

4. Next it decides the weight of the box.

5. It does the same job until it is given a new job.

FIRST LISTENING Page 42

Lecturer: When people think about a robot, they often picture a machine that looks something like a human being. However, that's not always the case! Most robots do not look much like a human being at all. They look like machines, because that's what most of them are—industrial machines. Today, I'm going to talk mostly about industrial robots used in industry. These are robots that do work that for humans would be physically demanding, repetitive, dangerous, or very boring.

Most industrial robots work on an assembly line in a factory. For example, a robot might put lids on jars of fruit or stack boxes for shipping. In a car factory, robotic arms on the assembly line join the parts of the car together. Other robots tighten the bolts on the car's wheels or paint the car. There are thousands of robots putting cars together in auto assembly plants. These robots are very precise when repeating a task. For example, they always tighten bolts with the same exact amount of force. They always move a heavy engine to exactly where it should be. And they always put a hole in the exact, same place in every car door, hour after hour. These are examples of robots doing the work humans could do, but the robots are doing the work more efficiently and precisely.

So, just how do robots work? To do its job, a robot first needs a control system. This control system directs the robot's mechanical parts. The control system of a robot is, so to speak, the robot's "brain." So how does a robot "learn" which action to do first and which of its moving parts needs to do that action?

The robot learns its job with the help and guidance of a human being. To teach an industrial robot to do something, first a person must use a handheld computer. The computer is used to guide the robot's "arm and hand" through the motions it needs to do. Then the robot stores the exact movements in its computer memory. The robot has sensors to gather information. So now, the robot will use its sensors to direct its actions. The robot "tells" its moving parts what to do and then it performs the action. For example, to pick up and move a box, the robot first finds the box. Next, it decides the weight of the box. Then it decides how much force is needed to lift and move the box. And finally, it finds the correct place to put the box down. It repeats the process over and over until it is turned off. It does the same job until it is given a new job and new program to follow.

Some scientists think that robots of the future will be smarter than today's robots. They may also look more humanlike, or even animallike. In fact, they may work and "think" more like humans do. The industrial robots we've been talking about so far today are automatic robots. They are known as "automatic" robots because they are programmed to follow a specific series of movements. Usually, they have parts that move, but they really don't travel around. On the other hand, an autonomous machine can change its behavior in relation to its surroundings. For example, an autonomous robot with wheels or legs to move around can change direction when it senses that there is something in its way. A robot such as Honda's famous ASIMO can detect the movements of people nearby. It can move to avoid bumping into someone coming toward it. ASIMO can even learn to dance by following the movements of a dancer next to it. I don't know whether or when people will welcome autonomous machines or humanlike robots. I guess that we will need to think about that in the future. We'll need to think about how we will interact with our robo-doctor, robo-teacher, robo-pet, or even our robo-friend. Think about that when you're doing your homework this evening. Would a robo-friend help you do your homework?

SECOND LISTENING Page 42

Today I'm going to talk mostly about industrial robots. • These robots do work that would be physically demanding, repetitive, dangerous, or very boring. • Most industrial robots work on an assembly line in a factory. • For example, a robot might put lids on jars of fruit or stack boxes for shipping. • In a car factory, robotic arms on the assembly line join the parts of the car together. • Other robots tighten the bolts on the car's wheels or paint the car. • There are thousands of robots putting cars together in auto assembly plants. • These robots are very precise when repeating a task. • They always tighten bolts with the same exact amount of force. • They always move a heavy engine to exactly where it should be. • They always put a hole in the exact, same place in every car door, hour after hour. • These are examples of robots doing the work humans could do. • But the robots are doing the work more efficiently and precisely. • So, just how do robots work? • To do its job, a robot first needs a control system. • This control system directs the robot's mechanical parts. • The control system of a robot is, so to speak, the robot's "brain." • How does a robot "learn" which action to do first? • How does it learn which of its moving parts needs to do that action? • The robot learns its job with the help and guidance of a human being. • To teach an industrial robot, first a person must use a handheld computer. • The computer is used to guide the robot's "arm and hand" through the motions it needs to do. • Then, the robot stores the movements in its computer memory. • The robot has sensors to gather information. • So now, the robot will use its sensors to direct its actions. • The robot "tells" its moving parts what to do, and then it performs the action. • First, it will find a box to be moved. • Next, it will decide the weight of the box. • Then it will decide how much force is needed to lift and move the box. • Finally, it will find the correct place to put the box down. • It repeats the process over and over, until it is turned off. • It does the same job until it is given a new job and new program to follow. • Some scientists think that robots of the future will be smarter than today's robots. • They may also look more humanlike, or even animallike. • In fact, they may even work and "think" more like humans do. • The industrial robots we've been talking about today are known as "automatic" robots. • They are known as "automatic" robots because they are programmed to follow specific movements. • Usually, they have parts that move, but they really don't travel around. • An autonomous machine can change its behavior in relation to its surroundings. • An autonomous robot with wheels or legs to move around can change direction. • It does this when it senses that there is an obstacle in its way. • A robot such as ASIMO can detect the movements of people nearby. • It can move to avoid something or someone coming toward it. • It can even learn to do dance by following the movements of a dancer next to it. • I do not know whether people will welcome autonomous machines or humanlike robots. • I guess that we will need to think about that in the future. • We'll need to think about how we will interact with humanlike robots—our robo-doctor, our robo-teacher, our robo-pet, or even our robo-friend.

THIRD LISTENING   Page 42

Part 1

Lecturer: When people think about a robot, they often picture a machine that looks something like a human being. However, that's not always the case! Most robots do not look much like a human being at all. They look like machines, because that's what most of them are—industrial machines. Today, I'm going to talk mostly about industrial robots used in industry. These are robots that do work that for humans would be physically demanding, repetitive, dangerous, or very boring.

Most industrial robots work on an assembly line in a factory. For example, a robot might put lids on jars of fruit or stack boxes for shipping. In a car factory, robotic arms on the assembly line join the parts of the car together. Other robots tighten the bolts on the car's wheels or paint the car. There are thousands of robots putting cars together in auto assembly plants. These robots are very precise when repeating a task. For example, they always tighten bolts with the same exact amount of force. They always move a heavy engine to exactly where it should be. And they always put a hole in the exact, same place in every car door, hour after hour. These are examples of robots doing the work humans could do, but the robots are doing the work more efficiently and precisely.

So, just how do robots work? To do it's job, a robot first needs a control system.

Part 2

See First Listening, above.

ACCURACY CHECK   Page 43

1. What kind of work do robots often do for people?
2. What do robots put lids on?
3. What does a robot first of all need to do its job?
4. What is the control system of an industrial robot?
5. How does an industrial robot learn to do its job?
6. When moving a box, what must the robot do first?

1. How does a robot learn to do its job?
2. Why are industrial robots known as automatic robots?

3. When moving forward, what does ASIMO do when something or someone is in its way?
4. What can ASIMO learn to do with the help of a dance partner?

EXPANSION TASK 1   Page 44

There are several steps you should follow when you do research. The first step is to look at previous research. You should read about other research that people have done and see if it can give you an idea for your own research.

Once you have your idea, design your experiment. Then you need to carry out your experiment carefully, making sure to make no mistakes.

The next step is to observe what happens.

After you have made your observations, put the results on your computer, analyze them, and write your research paper.

Finally, you should tell people what you did, what you saw, and what your analysis tells you.

EXPANSION TASK 2   Page 45

For this experiment, you will need an empty glass bottle. Write *bottle* next to its picture.

You will also need some vinegar. Vinegar is a liquid that is often used in cooking. It is an acid that people sometimes combine with an oil to put on salad. Write *vinegar*—V-I-N-E-G-A-R—next to its picture.

You will also need a funnel for this experiment. A funnel is a tool into which you can pour liquids or small solids, like rice or sugar, when you want to go from one container to another. Write *funnel*—F-U-N-N-E-L—next to its picture.

You will need some baking soda, too. Baking soda is a white substance that is often used in cooking, especially to make things rise. Write *baking soda* next to its picture.

Finally, you will need a balloon. Write *balloon* next to its picture.

First, pour some vinegar into the bottle until it is about one-quarter full. Next, use the funnel to pour some baking soda into the balloon. After that, carefully stretch the balloon over the neck of the bottle. Make sure you don't spill any baking soda into the bottle! Next, pick up the heavy part of the balloon so that the baking soda falls into the bottle.

When the baking soda mixes with the vinegar, a chemical reaction, or change, occurs. The reaction releases a gas, carbon dioxide. This is the same gas that is released when you open a can of carbonated soda. So when the vinegar and baking soda start mixing together, the balloon inflates, that is it gets bigger as it fills with the carbon dioxide gas.

Classification

CHAPTER 7

A Tidal Wave: What Is It? Can We Predict It?

VOCABULARY PREVIEW   Page 51

1. A tidal wave is a very large and destructive wall of water.
2. A tidal wave comes rushing in suddenly and unexpectedly at any time.
3. Do you know that tidal waves are not caused by storms?
4. When an earthquake takes place under the ocean, the ocean floor shakes and trembles.
5. Sometimes the ocean floor shifts during an underwater earthquake.
6. A double-wave tsunami can also be called a merging tsunami.
7. In 2011, a massive earthquake occurred off the coast of Japan.
8. A tsunami caused a crisis at a nuclear plant in northeastern Japan.
9. Today scientists can predict that a tidal wave will hit land.
10. It is possible to warn people that a tidal wave is coming.

NOTETAKING PREPARATION   Page 52

1. A tidal wave is different from a wave that is caused by a tide.
2. A *tsunami* is another name for a tidal wave.
3. A double tsunami is two tidal waves coming together.
4. Very big waves that occur out at sea are not tidal waves.

1. A tidal wave is a very large and destructive wave.
2. To *quake* means to move up and down very quickly or to shake.

3. A true tide can be defined as the normal rise and fall of ocean water at regular times each day.
4. A seismograph is a type of instrument for measuring earthquakes.

FIRST LISTENING   Page 53

Lecturer: Today our lecture is about tidal waves. I'll define what a tidal wave is, and what a tidal wave is not. I'll also define some other terms related to tidal waves.

So what is a tidal wave? A tidal wave is a very large and very destructive wall of water. This wall of water rushes in from the ocean toward the land. Scientists use the Japanese word *tsunami* to describe these waves. In Japanese, *tsunami* actually means "harbor wave." You see, the waves are tallest when they reach a harbor, which is an area of the ocean just before the land, where boats are kept.

Now, normal waves are caused by tides or storms over the water. But did you know that tidal waves are not caused by storms, and that tidal waves are not really tides at all? A true tide can be defined as the regular rise and fall of ocean waters, at definite times each day. A tidal wave, or tsunami, comes rushing in suddenly and unexpectedly at any time. It could come rushing in during the morning, in the afternoon, or during the night.

A tidal wave is caused by an underwater earthquake. To *quake* means to move up and down or from side to side very quickly. To *quake* also means "to shake" or "to tremble." When an earthquake takes place under the ocean, the ocean floor shakes and trembles, and sometimes the ocean floor shifts. That is, the ocean floor moves. It is this shifting of the ocean floor that produces the tidal wave. The earth and water move, causing a tidal wave. The tidal wave begins to move across the sea at great speed.

In 2011, a massive earthquake occurred off the coast of Japan. The quake caused a double-wave tsunami. A double-wave tsunami can also be called a *merging tsunami*. When a merging, or double-wave, tsunami occurs, two very large waves combine. This increases the destruction when the tidal wave reaches land.

Tsunamis have taken many lives in the past. For instance, the tsunami caused by a 9.0 magnitude earthquake off the coast of Japan on March 11, 2011, took the lives of more than 20,000 people. The tsunami also destroyed large areas of northeastern Japan, and it caused a crisis at a nuclear plant. This was a terrible disaster.

Today scientists can predict that a tidal wave will hit land. These scientists use a seismograph. A seismograph is a type of instrument that records the strength, direction, and length of an earthquake. The seismograph tells the scientists if the earthquake under the ocean is likely to cause a tidal wave. So although it is not possible to stop a tidal wave, it is possible to warn people that a tidal wave is coming. This warning can save many lives.

SECOND LISTENING Page 53

A tidal wave is a very large wall of water. • It is a very destructive wall of water. • The water rushes in from the ocean toward the land. • Scientists use the Japanese word *tsunami* to describe these waves. • In Japanese, *tsunami* means "harbor wave." • The waves are tallest when they reach a harbor. • A harbor is an area of the ocean just before the land, where boats are kept. • Normal waves are caused by tides or storms. • Tidal waves are not caused by storms. • And tidal waves are not really tides at all. • A true tide is the regular rise and fall of ocean water at definite times each day. • A tidal wave comes rushing in suddenly and unexpectedly at any time. • It could come in the morning, in the afternoon, or during the night. • A tidal wave is caused by an underwater earthquake. • To *quake* means to move up and down or from side to side very quickly. • To *quake* also means "to shake" or "to tremble." • When an earthquake takes place under the ocean, the ocean floor shakes and trembles. • Sometimes the ocean floor shifts. • That is, the ocean floor moves. • Shifting of the ocean floor produces the tidal wave. • The earth and water move, causing a tidal wave. • The tidal wave moves across the sea. • It moves at great speed. • In 2011, a massive earthquake occurred off the coast of Japan. • The quake caused a double-wave tsunami. • A double-wave tsunami can also be defined as a *merging tsunami*. • When a merging tsunami occurs, two very, very large waves combine. • This increases the destruction when the tidal wave reaches land. • Tsunamis have taken many lives in the past. • A tsunami was caused by a 9.0 magnitude earthquake on March 11, 2011. • It took the lives of more than 20,000 people. • The tsunami also destroyed large areas of northeastern Japan. • It caused a crisis at a nuclear plant. • This was a terrible disaster. • Today scientists can predict that a tidal wave will hit land. • They use a seismograph. • It records the strength and the direction of an earthquake. • A seismograph also records the length of time of an earthquake. • It tells the scientists if an earthquake under the ocean could cause a tidal wave. • It is not possible to stop a tidal wave. • It is possible to warn people that a tidal wave is coming. • This warning can save many lives.

THIRD LISTENING Page 53

Part 1

Lecturer: Today our lesson is about tidal waves. I'll define what a tidal wave is, and what a tidal wave is not. I'll also define some other terms related to tidal waves.

So what is a tidal wave? A tidal wave is a very large and very destructive wall of water. This wall of water rushes in from the ocean toward the land. Scientists use the Japanese word *tsunami* to describe these waves. In Japanese, "tsunami" actually means "harbor wave." You see, the waves are tallest when they reach a harbor, which is an area of the ocean just before the land, where boats are kept.

Now, normal waves are caused by tides or storms over the water. But did you know that tidal waves are not caused by storms, and that tidal waves are not really tides at all? A true tide can be defined as the regular rise and fall of ocean waters, at definite times each day. A tidal wave, or tsunami, comes rushing in suddenly and unexpectedly at any time. It could come rushing in during the morning, in the afternoon, or during the night.

A tidal wave is caused by an underwater earthquake.

Part 2

See First Listening, above.

ACCURACY CHECK Page 54

1. What is a tidal wave?
2. What does the Japanese word *tsunami* mean?
3. What is the name for an area of the ocean just before the land, where boats are kept?
4. What do we call the regular rise and fall of ocean waters at definite times each day?
5. What is caused by an underwater earthquake?
6. During an underwater earthquake, what shakes, trembles, and sometimes shifts?
7. When two very large waves combine, what do they form?
8. What instrument records the strength, the direction, and the length of time of earthquakes?

EXPANSION TASK 1 Page 55

1 Across It is a type of instrument that measures the strength of an earthquake. The answer is *seismograph*—S-E-I-S-M-O-G-R-A-P-H.

1 Down This weather event may be defined as a heavy fall of rain or snow with much wind.

2 Down This means to change position, like the ocean floor after an earthquake.

3 Down When people guess what may happen, they do this.

4 Across These are formed by the motion of ocean water and are sometimes very large.

5 Down This type of large wave is caused by an earthquake under the ocean.

6 Down   It is the regular rise and fall of the ocean at different times each day.

7 Across These people collect and study scientific information.

7 Down   It may be defined as a small ocean.

8 Across This means to tell someone that danger is coming.

 B

1 Down   A weather event that may be defined as a heavy fall of rain or snow with much wind is a <u>storm</u>. S-T-O-R-M

2 Down   To change position, like the ocean floor after an earthquake, is to <u>shift</u>. S-H-I-F-T

3 Down   When people guess what may happen, they <u>predict</u>. P-R-E-D-I-C-T

4 Across The motion of ocean water forms <u>waves</u>, which are sometimes very large. W-A-V-E-S

5 Down   A large wave caused by an earthquake under the ocean is a <u>tsunami</u>. T-S-U-N-A-M-I

6 Down   The regular rise and fall of the ocean at different times each day is the <u>tide</u>. T-I-D-E

7 Across People who collect and study scientific information are <u>scientists</u>. S-C-I-E-N-T-I-S-T-S

7 Down   A small ocean is a <u>sea</u>. S-E-A

8 Across To tell someone that danger is coming is to <u>warn</u>. W-A-R-N

EXPANSION TASK 2   Page 55

Natural disasters are sometimes divided into four main categories: (1) geological disasters, (2) meteorological disasters, (3) hydrological disasters, and (4) space disasters.

Geological disasters include earthquakes, volcanoes, and landslides. In 1958, in Alaska, a large earthquake caused a major landslide. About 100 million tons of rock crashed into a bay in Alaska. This landslide caused the largest ever tsunami with a 1,700-foot-high wave that crashed into land on the opposite side of the bay. Amazingly, no one was killed.

Meteorological disasters are related to the weather. Such disasters include electrical storms, heat waves, hurricanes, and tornados. A tornado is a column of air that turns around and around very fast. It can have wind speeds of 300 miles an hour. It can touch the earth and travel dozens of miles. It can blow away anything in its path, including people, cars, animals, houses, and trees. A deadly tornado occurred in the small country of Bangladesh in 1989. This tornado killed more than 1,300 people.

A flood is an example of a hydrologic disaster. *Hydrologic* means it involves water. One very disastrous flood occurred in China back in 1887. It was known as the 1887 Yellow River Flood. It is believed that this flood took the lives of as many as two million people.

The fourth category is space disasters. Space disasters occur when something from outer space—such as an asteroid or comet—hits the earth. In 1908, an asteroid hit a forest in Russia. It caused a huge explosion and destroyed many trees. Fortunately, it was very far from a town or a city. No one is sure how many people died.

 CHAPTER 8

Levels of Language: Formal and Informal

VOCABULARY PREVIEW   Page 57

 A

1. Today I want to talk about levels of language usage.

2. Formal written language is the kind you find in reference books such as encyclopedias.

3. People usually use formal English at ceremonies such as graduations.

4. We also tend to use formal language in conversations with persons we don't know well.

5. Formal language tends to be more polite.

6. Informal language is used in conversation with colleagues, family, and friends.

7. I might say to a friend, "Close the door, please." To someone in authority I would say, "Excuse me, could you please close the door?"

8. The difference between formal and informal usage can be learned by observing and interacting with native speakers.

NOTETAKING PREPARATION   Page 58

 A

Another difference between formal and informal language is some of the vocabulary. There are some words and phrases that belong in formal language and others that are informal. Let me give you a couple of examples of what I mean. Let's say that I really like soccer. If I'm talking to my friend or colleague, I might say, "I'm just crazy about soccer!" But if I were talking to my boss or a friend of my parents, I would probably say, "I really enjoy soccer" or "I like soccer very much."

B

1. An e-mail to a boss, for instance, is usually written in a formal style.

2. Let me give you an example of what I mean by informal.

3. Words and phrases such as *please, would you mind,* and *if you'd be so kind* are formal language.

4. Some phrases are informal while others are formal. For example, *I get it* is informal, but *I see what you mean* is formal.

5. One example is a news report on television.

FIRST LISTENING   Page 59

Lecturer: Today I want to talk about levels of language usage. You probably have noticed that people express similar ideas in different ways, depending on the situation they are in. This is very natural. All languages have two general, broad categories, or levels, of usage: a formal level and an informal level. And this is true for English, too. I'm not talking about correct and incorrect English. What I'm talking about are two levels of correct English. Each level is correct when used in a particular situation.

Formal language is the kind of language you find in textbooks, reference books such as encyclopedias, and in business letters. For example, a letter to a university would be in a formal style. You would also use formal English in essays and papers that you write in school. People usually use formal English when they give classroom lectures or speeches at ceremonies such as graduations. We also tend to use formal language in conversations with people we don't know well or with people we have a formal relationship with, such as professors, bosses, doctors, friends of our parents', strangers, etc. Informal language is used in conversation with colleagues, family, and friends, and when we write personal notes, e-mails, or text messages to friends.

Formal language is different from informal language in several ways. However, today I'm just going to talk about a couple of ways. First of all, formal language tends to be more polite. Interestingly, formal language usually takes more words to be polite. For example, I might say to a friend or family member, "Close the door, please," but to a stranger or someone in authority I probably would say something like "Would you mind closing the door?" or "Excuse me, could you please close the door?" Using words like "could" and "would" makes my request sound more polite, as well as more formal. With friends and family, I want to be polite, so I use the word "please." But I don't want to sound too formal, so I don't use phrases like "Would you" or "Excuse me."

Another difference between formal and informal language is some of the vocabulary. There are some words and phrases that belong in formal language and others that are informal. Let me give you a couple of examples of what I mean. Let's say that I really like soccer. If I'm talking to my friend or colleague, I might say, "I'm just crazy about soccer!" But if I were talking

to my boss or a friend of my parents', I would probably say, "I really enjoy soccer" or "I like soccer very much." Or let's say I'm telling someone some news I heard about the police. To my friend I might call the police "the cops." But to my teacher I would say, "the police."

The line between formal and informal language is not always clear, and people are probably less formal today than in the past. But it is useful to be aware that these two levels, or categories, do exist. The best way for a nonnative speaker of English to learn the difference is to observe the different ways English speakers speak or write in different situations. The speech of television news reporters, your college professors in class, your doctors in their offices, etc., will usually be more formal. However, the speech of your classmates, teammates, family members, and friends will generally be more informal. The difference can be learned over time by observing and interacting with native or near-native speakers of English.

SECOND LISTENING   Page 59

All languages have two general levels of usage: • A formal level and an informal level. • They are two levels of correct English. • Each level is correct when used in a particular situation. • Formal language is used in textbooks and reference books. • It is used in business letters. • It is used in compositions and essays you write in school. • People use formal English in lectures and speeches at ceremonies. • We tend to use formal language in conversations with people we don't know well. • We use it with people we have formal relationships with. • We have formal relationships with professors, bosses, and doctors. • We have formal relationships with friends of our parents and strangers. • Informal English is used in conversation with colleagues, family, and friends. • Informal English is used when we write notes, e-mails, or text messages to friends. • Formal language is different from informal language. • It is different in several ways. • First, formal language is more polite. • Formal politeness usually takes more words. • Words like "could" and "would" sound polite and formal. • Some of the words and phrases in formal and informal English are different. • To my friend I might say, "I'm just crazy about soccer!" • To my boss I would probably say, "I really enjoy" or "I really like soccer." • To my friend I might call the police "the cops." • But to my teacher I would say, "the police." • The line between formal and informal language is not always clear. • And people are probably less formal today than in the past. • But it is useful to be aware that these two levels, or categories, do exist. • The best way for a nonnative speaker of English to learn the difference is to observe. • Observe the way different people use English in different situations. • The speech of television news reporters, college professors, and doctors will be formal. • The speech of classmates, teammates, family members, and friends will be informal. • The difference can be learned by observing and interacting with native speakers.

THIRD LISTENING Page 59

Part 1

Lecturer: Today I want to talk about levels of language usage. You probably have noticed that people express similar ideas in different ways, depending on the situation they are in. This is very natural. All languages have two general, broad categories, or levels, of usage: a formal level and an informal level. And this is true for English, too. I'm not talking about correct and incorrect English. What I'm talking about are two levels of correct English. Each level is correct when used in a particular situation.

Formal language is the kind of language you find in textbooks, reference books such as encyclopedias, and in business letters. For example, a letter to a university would be in a formal style. You would also use formal English in essays and papers that you write in school. People usually use formal English when they give classroom lectures or speeches at ceremonies such as graduations. We also tend to use formal language in conversations with people we don't know well or with people we have a formal relationship with, such as professors, bosses, doctors, friends of our parents', strangers, etc. Informal language is used in conversation with colleagues, family, and friends, and when we write personal notes, e-mails, or text messages to friends.

Part 2

See First Listening, above.

ACCURACY CHECK Page 60

1. Which type of writing is usually written in formal English?
2. Which people do we usually speak to using informal language?
3. What would be the most formal way to request some salt?
4. Which sentence should *not* be in a formal paper you write for a class?
5. It's unusual to find both formal and informal levels of usage in a language.
6. All languages have two general, broad categories, or levels of usage: formal and informal.
7. People usually use formal language when they meet someone for the first time.
8. The best way to learn the difference between formal and informal English is to look up every new word in the dictionary.

EXPANSION TASK 1 Page 61

1. He won the game by two points.
   He lost the game by one point.
2. She's feeling blue.
   She's wearing blue.
3. I can't bear to lose.
   He saw a bear.
4. I don't eat meat any more.
   We don't meet any more.
5. The wind blew hard.
   Blue is my favorite color.
6. She's very honest and never tells a lie.
   She went to lie down because she's very tired.
7. We're looking for a male actor for this role.
   I'm waiting for the mail to arrive.
8. I don't think you're right.
   I think you have to turn right.
9. She has very fair skin and hair.
   She didn't have the right fare for the bus.

See A, above.

EXPANSION TASK 2 Page 62

1. *Nouns* are words that are defined as people, places, things, or ideas. There are three types of nouns: concrete, abstract, and proper nouns. A concrete noun is something you can see and touch. For example, *desk* and *banana* are both concrete nouns. An abstract noun is a noun you cannot see or touch. For example, *love* is an abstract noun. Proper nouns are names of specific people and places. For example, *India* and *Michael* are both proper nouns.

2. *Verbs* are words that describe an action or a state of being. There are two types of verbs, *active* and *state* verbs. Active verbs describe an action that occurs. For example, *run* and *talk* are both active verbs. State verbs are verbs that describe a state of being. For example, *be* and *seem* are both state verbs.

3. *Adverbs* are words or phrases that provide extra information about verbs. There are three types of adverbs: adverbs of place, adverbs of time, and adverbs of manner. Adverbs of place tell you *where* something happened. For example, *in the garden* is an adverb of place. Adverbs of time tell you *when* something happened, for example, *in the afternoon*. Adverbs of manner tell you *how* something happened, for example, *slowly* or *well*.

CHAPTER 9

Power: The Kinds of Power People Use and Abuse

VOCABULARY PREVIEW Page 64

A

1. We all wish to avoid uncomfortable emotions.
2. People who have information can manipulate those who do not have this information.
3. Some people may identify with a particular friend, or, say, a rock star.
4. Many people imitate and are controlled by the people they identify with.
5. Referent power can be used for good or evil purposes.
6. Often a person admires or wants to behave like a particular person.
7. Government officials usually exercise legitimate power.
8. Some experts use their expertise to gain power.
9. Reward, or coercive, power is used to reward or punish people's actions or behavior.

NOTETAKING PREPARATION Page 65

A

1. The fifth type of power is reward, or coercive, power.
2. Expert power is one more variety of power.
3. Power is made up of five different categories.
4. The first type of power is called information power.
5. There are two more classes of power: referent power and legitimate power.

B

1. The final class of power is reward power.
2. Another type of power is referent power.
3. A third variety of power is classified as legitimate power.
4. The next kind of power is expert power.
5. The first sort of power is information power.

FIRST LISTENING Page 66

Lecturer: What is power? This is what I will be talking to you about today.

Well, one social psychologist defines power as "the ability to determine or to change the actions of other people." He calls the need for a sense of power one of the primary forces in human life. He also writes that a feeling that you have no power is a very uncomfortable feeling for everyone. And since we all wish to avoid uncomfortable emotions, we try to use power to influence others.

So, what exactly is power? Social psychologists have identified five basic categories of power. These include the following: (1) information power; (2) referent power; (3) legitimate power; (4) expert power; and finally, (5) reward or coercive power. Now, I'd like to talk briefly about each of these types in the next few minutes, and I'll give some specific examples of each.

The first type of power is called information power. Some psychologists believe that information power is one of the most effective types of power and control. The person who has information that other people want and need, but do not have, is definitely in a position of power. Why is this? Well, most people like to receive and have information. Having information increases a person's own sense of power. People who have or give information can manipulate those who do not have this information. Often, when people receive information, they don't know that they are being manipulated by those who provided the information. For example, newspapers, magazines, and articles on the Web provide a lot of information. And the people who read information in the media often believe what they read, even when many reports, especially on the Internet, may not be accurate.

A second variety of power is known as referent power. Often a person admires or wants to behave like a particular person, or the members of a particular group. For example, some people may want to behave like or support the members of a soccer team or a group of friends. Some people may identify strongly with and want to be like a particular friend, or, say, a rock star. If you identify with another person, that person has power over you, and that person can influence your actions and behavior. Many people imitate and are controlled by the people they identify with. Let me give you a sad example of the use of this type of power for evil purposes. In Jonestown, Guyana, more than 900 people committed suicide when their religious leader, Jim Jones, told them to kill themselves. They did what he told them to do because he had referent power over them. They identified with him; they believed in him, and they did what he told them to do. What a tragedy! Referent power can be used for good or evil purposes. So we need to be aware of those who have referent power over us.

A third kind of power is classified as legitimate power. Government officials usually exercise a so-called legitimate power. For example, when the government decides to raise taxes on people, or go to war, most people (but not all) will do what their government officials tell them to do. Police as well as soldiers have a lot of legitimate power. One psychologist reported on an experiment that showed an example of this type of power. In this experiment, a researcher asked people on the street to move away from a bus stop. When he was dressed in everyday clothes, few people followed his request to move away from the bus stop. When the researcher was dressed in a uniform, most people followed his request and moved away from the bus stop. The uniform seemed to give the young researcher a look of legitimate power. And people obeyed him when they saw the uniform.

A fourth class of power is known as expert power. An expert is a person who is very skilled in some area, such as in science or sports. When a person knows a lot about something, such as computers or cars, many people are impressed by the person's knowledge and expertise. Some of these "experts" use their skills and knowledge to gain power and influence. Or they use it to gain money or admiration. In other words, they use their expertise to gain power.

Finally, the fifth type of power is called reward, or coercive, power. This type of power is used by people who can reward or punish another person's actions or behavior. Giving a reward will change people's behavior because it offers people a chance to gain something. Giving a punishment may or may not cause people to do what the powerful person wants them to do. Changes may not last very long. The person who uses coercive power may also have to watch carefully that the less powerful person does, in fact, change his or her actions or behavior.

To sum up, then, power comes in many forms. It may come from having information that other people want or need; it may come from being a referent for other people to identify with or to imitate; it may come from having an official, or legitimate, position of authority, like a teacher in a classroom; it may come from having skills or expertise; or it may come from the power to reward or punish. It is important to be aware then that people will try to exercise one or more of these kinds of power over us throughout our lives.

SECOND LISTENING   Page 66

Power is "the ability to determine or change the actions of other people." • We try to use power to influence others. • Social psychologists identify five basic categories of power. • These categories include information power and referent power. • They also include legitimate power, expert power, and reward or coercive power. • Information power is one of the most effective types of power and control. • The person who has information that other people want is in a position of power. • People like to receive and have information. • Having information increases a person's own sense of power. • People who have information can manipulate those who do not have information. • Often when people receive information they don't know they are being

manipulated. • Newspapers, magazines, and articles on the Web provide a lot of information. • People who read information in the media often believe the information they read. • Many reports, especially on the Internet, may not be accurate. • A second variety of power is referent power. • Often a person admires or wants to behave like a particular person. • If you identify with another person, that person has power over you. • That person can influence your actions and behavior. • Many people imitate and are controlled by people they identify with. • In Jonestown, Guyana, 900 people committed suicide. • Their religious leader told them to kill themselves. • He had referent power over them. • They identified with him and they did what he told them to do. • We need to be aware of those who have referent power over us. • Government officials exercise legitimate power. • Most people will do what their government officials tell them to do. • Police as well as soldiers have a lot of legitimate power. • An experiment showed an example of legitimate power. • A researcher asked people on the street to move away from a bus stop. • When he was dressed in everyday clothes, few people moved away from the bus stop. • When he dressed in a uniform, most people moved away from the bus stop. • The uniform seemed to give the young researcher a look of legitimate power. • People obeyed him when they saw the uniform. • A fourth class of power is expert power. • An expert is a person who is skilled in some area. • People are impressed by a person's knowledge and expertise. • Some experts use their skills to gain power, influence, money, and admiration. • They use their expertise to gain power. • Reward, or coercive, power is used to reward or punish people's actions or behavior. • Giving a reward will change people's behavior. • A reward offers people a chance for gain. • Giving a punishment may not cause people to do what the powerful person wants. • The person who uses coercive power may also have to watch carefully. • The person must watch that the less powerful person does change. • Power comes in many forms. • Power may come from having information people want or need. • Power may come from being a referent for other people. • Power may come from having a position of authority. • Power may come from having skill or expertise. • Power may come from having the power to reward or punish. • It is important to be aware. • People will try to exercise one or more of these kinds of power over us.

THIRD LISTENING   Page 66

Part 1

Lecturer: What is power? This is what I will be talking to you about today.

Well, one social psychologist defines power as "the ability to determine or to change the actions of other people." He calls the need for a sense of power one of the primary forces in human life. He also writes that a feeling that you have no power is a very uncomfortable feeling for everyone. And since we all wish to avoid uncomfortable emotions, we try to use power to influence others.

So, what exactly is power? Social psychologists have identified five basic categories of power. These include the following: (1) information power; (2) referent power; (3) legitimate power; (4) expert power; and finally, (5) reward or coercive power. Now I'd like to talk briefly about each of these types in the next few minutes, and I'll give some specific examples of each.

The first type of power is called information power. Some psychologists believe that information power is one of the most effective types of power and control. The person who has information that other people want and need, but do not have, is definitely in a position of power. Why is this? Well, most people like to receive and have information. Having information increases a person's own sense of power. People who have or give information can manipulate those who do not have this information. Often, when people receive information, they don't know that they are being manipulated by those who provided the information. For example, newspapers, magazines, and articles on the Web provide a lot of information. And the people who read information in the media often believe what they read, even when many reports, especially on the Internet, may not be accurate.

Part 2

See First Listening, above.

ACCURACY CHECK Page 67

1. What kind of power do Web articles provide to those who read them?
2. If a teenager wishes to act like a favorite rock singer, which type of power does that singer have over the teenager?
3. Which kind of power may or may not lead to changes that the person in power wants and requires?
4. When a government decides to raise taxes on a product like gas, what kind of power is being used?
5. Some psychologists believe that information power is one of the most effective types of power.
6. The experiment using a man dressed as a guard gave an example of information power.
7. Coercive power may not have a lasting effect.
8. An expert is a person who is very skilled in some area.
9. We use power to manipulate other people, and others try to manipulate us.

EXPANSION TASK 1 Page 68

1. A *mammal* is a warm-blooded animal. It can live on the land or in water. It breathes oxygen from the air. When the babies are born, the mother feeds her young with milk from her body.
2. A *bird* is a warm-blooded animal. It breathes oxygen from the air. It has two legs and instead of having two arms, it has two wings with feathers. Birds live on land, but can go in water. Their young come from eggs that the mother bird lays.
3. A *fish* is a cold-blooded animal. It lives its entire life in water. It cannot live on land because it gets its oxygen from the water, not the air. Most fish lay eggs, but not all. In some fish, the young come straight from the mother's body. Fish do not have arms or legs to move them through the water. They have fins.
4. A *reptile* is a cold-blooded animal. It crawls or moves on its stomach or on small short legs. It can live on land or in the water. But even reptiles that live in the water must get their oxygen from the air. Like birds, reptiles lay eggs.
5. An *amphibian* is a cold-blooded animal. It starts its life in the water. When it is young, it gets oxygen from water, but as it gets older, it moves onto land and gets oxygen from the air. Most amphibians lay eggs.

EXPANSION TASK 2 Page 69

1. This animal is warm-blooded. It lives on the land. It has four legs and a long tail and can be used as transportation by humans. What is it? Write number 1 on the picture of this animal.
2. This animal is cold-blooded. It lives both on land and in water. It has four legs and it lays eggs. It has big sharp teeth and can be very dangerous to humans. What is it? Write number 2 on the picture of this animal.
3. This animal is warm-blooded. It lives on the land. It has legs, but no arms. Instead, it has feathers and wings for flying. It is sometimes the symbol of American freedom. What is it? Write number 3 on the picture of this animal.
4. This animal is cold-blooded. It lives only in the water. It has very sharp teeth and can sometimes be very large. What is it? Write number 4 on the picture of this animal.
5. This animal lives in the water, but it gets its oxygen from the air. It is warm-blooded and can be very, very large. It has no arms or legs. What is it? Write number 5 on the picture of this animal.

6. This animal is born in the water, but when it's grown, it can breathe air and lives near water, not in it. It's a small animal that has strong back legs and moves along the ground with big jumps. What is it? Write number 6 on the picture of this animal.

7. This animal has no arms or legs and moves along the ground. It is cold-blooded, and it lays eggs. It can be poisonous and can kill a person with its bite. What is it? Write number 7 on the picture of this animal.

8. This animal is warm-blooded. It lives on land and in the water. It has feathers and wings, but it can swim underwater. What is it? Write number 8 on the picture of this animal.

1. This animal is a horse. H-O-R-S-E. It's a mammal.
2. This animal is an alligator. A-L-L-I-G-A-T-O-R. It's a reptile.
3. This is an eagle. E-A-G-L-E. It's a bird.
4. This is a shark. S-H-A-R-K. It's a fish.
5. This animal is a whale. W-H-A-L-E. It's a mammal.
6. This is a frog. F-R-O-G. It is an amphibian.
7. This animal is a snake. S-N-A-K-E. It belongs to the reptile class.
8. This animal is a penguin. P-E-N-G-U-I-N. It's a bird.

UNIT 4

Comparison and Contrast

CHAPTER 10

Asian and African Elephants: Similarities and Differences

VOCABULARY PREVIEW Page 75

1. Today's topic is the largest land mammals on earth—elephants.
2. Elephants are enormous animals.
3. An elephant sometimes uses its trunk to put grasses, leaves, and water into its mouth.
4. Elephants can be trained to do heavy work.
5. The Asian elephant sometimes does not have any tusks at all.
6. A big difference between the two types of elephants is their temperament.
7. The Asian elephant is tamer than the African elephant.

8. The African elephant is much wilder than the Asian elephant.
9. There certainly are differences between the African and the Asian elephants, but they are both fascinating animals.

NOTETAKING PREPARATION Page 76

There are two main types of camels in the world today. One is the two-humped, or dromedary, camel, spelled D-R-O-M-E-D-A-R-Y. The other is the one-humped, or Bactrian, camel. That is spelled B-A-C-T-R-I-A-N. The dromedary camel lives mostly in the desert countries of North Africa and the Middle East, while the Bactrian camel lives in Central Asia. Both camels are similar in height, but the Bactrian usually is a little heavier and has much shorter legs. Both types of camels are fully domesticated animals, like cows, although a few wild camels are reported still to be living in groups in Central Asia. All camels have a unique feature, which is that they have three stomachs and can go many days without drinking water.

Let's start with some similarities. Well, for one thing, both animals have trunks. An elephant uses its trunk to put grasses, leaves, and water into its mouth. Typically, elephants drink about 50 gallons of water each day. Both kinds of elephants use their trunks to pick up very small objects and very large, heavy objects. They can even pick up trees with their trunks. Another similarity is that both animals are intelligent. Both animals can be trained to do heavy work. They can also be trained to do tricks to entertain people. In other words, they can do work for people, and they can also be taught to entertain people.

FIRST LISTENING Page 77

Lecturer: Today's topic has to do with the largest land mammals on earth—elephants. You probably know what the largest mammal in the sea is, right? Whales. However on land, elephants are the largest mammals. There are two types of elephants. One is the Asian elephant of India and Southeast Asia; the other is the African elephant. These two types of elephants are enormous mammals.

So all elephants are very large, but as I said, there are two types of elephants, African and the Asian. I'm going to compare and contrast the similarities and differences between the two species for you today.

Let's start with some similarities. Well, for one thing, both animals have trunks. An elephant uses its trunk to put grasses, leaves, and water into its mouth. Typically, elephants drink about 50 gallons of water each day. Both kinds of elephants use their trunks to pick up very small objects and very large, heavy objects. They can even pick up trees with their trunks. Another similarity is that both animals are intelligent. Both animals can be trained to do heavy work. They can also be trained to do tricks to entertain people. In other words, they can do work for people, and they can also be taught to entertain people.

As I said before, the African and the Asian elephants are alike in many ways, but they are also quite different, too. Let me explain what I mean.

The African elephant is larger and heavier than the Asian elephant. Asian elephants reach a height of about 10 feet, and African elephants reach about 13 feet tall. The African male elephant weighs between 12,000 and 14,000 pounds. In contrast, the average Asian male elephant weighs between 7,000 and 12,000 pounds. So one is bigger than the other, but as you can see both are still enormous animals.

Another difference between the two kinds of elephants is the size of the ears. Asian elephants have smaller ears than the African elephants. The African elephant has two very large teeth. These teeth are called tusks. The Asian elephant, however, sometimes does not have any tusks at all. The elephants differ in color, too. The African elephant is dark gray in color, while the Asian elephant is light gray. Occasionally an Asian elephant is even white! The last big difference between the two types of elephants is their temperament. The Asian elephant is tamer than the African elephant. Or put another way, the African elephant is much wilder than the Asian elephant. As a result, it is more difficult to train the African elephant to perform tricks to entertain people. That's why the elephants you see in the circus are probably Asian elephants and not African elephants.

Yes, there certainly are differences between the African and the Asian elephants, but as I mentioned at the start of my talk, there is one big similarity between the two animals: they are both fascinating, and enormous, animals.

SECOND LISTENING   Page 77

The largest land mammals on earth are elephants. • There are two types of elephants. • One is the Asian elephant of India and Southeast Asia. • The other is the African elephant. • These two types of elephants are enormous mammals. • All elephants are very large. • But there are two types of elephants, African and Asian. • I'm going to compare and contrast the similarities and differences between the two species. • Let's start with some similarities. • Both animals have trunks. • An elephant uses its trunk to put grasses, leaves, and water into its mouth. • Elephants drink about 50 gallons of water each day. • Elephants use their trunks to pick up very small objects and very large, heavy objects. • Both animals can be trained to work for people. • Both can

be trained to do tricks. • What are the differences? • The African elephant is larger and heavier than the Asian elephant. • Asian elephants reach a height of about 10 feet. • African elephants reach about 13 feet tall. • The African male elephant weighs between 12,000 and 14,000 pounds. • The average Asian male elephant weighs between 7,000 and 12,000 pounds. • So one is bigger than the other. • But both are enormous animals. • Asian elephants have smaller ears than African elephants. • The African elephant has two very large teeth. • These teeth are called tusks. • The Asian elephant sometimes does not have any tusks. • The African elephant is dark gray in color. • The Asian elephant is light gray. • Occasionally an Asian elephant is even white. • The Asian elephant is tamer than the African elephant. • The African elephant is much wilder than the Asian elephant. • The elephants you see in the circus are probably Asian elephants.

THIRD LISTENING   Page 77

Part 1

Lecturer: Today's topic has to do with the largest land mammals on earth—elephants. You probably know what the largest mammal in the sea is, right? Whales. However on land, elephants are the largest mammals. There are two types of elephants. One is the Asian elephant of India and Southeast Asia; the other is the African elephant. These two types of elephants are enormous mammals.

So all elephants are very large, but as I said, there are two types of elephants, African and the Asian. I'm going to compare and contrast the similarities and differences between the two species for you today.

Let's start with some other similarities. Well, for one thing, both animals have trunks. An elephant uses its trunk to put grasses, leaves, and water into its mouth. Typically, elephants drink about 50 gallons of water each day. Both kinds of elephants use their trunks to pick up very small objects and very large, heavy objects. They can even pick up trees with their trunks. Another similarity is that both animals are intelligent. Both animals can be trained to do heavy work. They can also be trained to do tricks to entertain people. In other words, they can do work for people, and they can also be taught to entertain people.

Part 2

See First Listening, above.

ACCURACY CHECK   Page 78

1. What part of an elephant's body does it use to put water in its mouth?

2. Which type of elephants can be trained to do heavy work for people?

3. What is the weight range for a male African elephant?

4. What best describes the size of the Asian elephant in comparison to the African elephant?

1. Elephants use their trunks to pick up small and large objects.

2. Elephants enjoy working and doing tricks for people.

3. African elephants are generally wilder than Asian elephants.

4. Asian elephants have smaller ears than African elephants.

5. Elephants drink 50 gallons of water each day.

EXPANSION TASK 1 Page 79

There are several similarities in appearance between the hippopotamus and the rhinoceros. Both are very big and heavy animals and mostly have a very similar gray color. The hippopotamus can weigh as much as 4,000 pounds or 1,800 kilograms. The rhinoceros can be even bigger— up to 9,000 pounds or 4,100 kilos.

One difference in appearance is that rhinos have a hump or bump on their shoulders and a horn on their nose. Actually some rhinos have two horns on their nose or snout.

The mouths of the animals are different, too. The mouth of the hippopotamus is huge, while the mouth of the rhino is quite small.

Considering they are such big animals, it is perhaps surprising to learn that hippos are excellent swimmers and can hold their breath under water for up to five minutes. Hippos, in fact, love to spend a lot of their time in the water. Rhinos, on the other hand, spend their time on land, on grassy plains or in dense tropical or semi-tropical forests, looking for food.

And what about their diet? What do hippos and rhinos eat? Both hippos and rhinos are herbivores, or plant eaters. The rhinoceros eats only plants. The hippo diet consists mainly of grasses and plants in and near the water. They do most of their eating at night. During the day, they rest and lie in the water to keep cool.

And where can we find these large creatures? Well, the hippo lives in Africa while rhinos are found both in Africa as well as Asia.

What can I say about their social behavior? Well, for one thing, hippos like the company of other hippos. They live in groups of up to 40 hippos. They're very social animals. What about the rhino? Well, let's just say they enjoy their own company and spend most of their time alone.

Let me end by saying that both the hippo and the rhino are very endangered animals in the wild. They may not be around in a hundred years, but let's hope they are.

EXPANSION TASK 2 Page 80

1. Both Charlie and David are married.

2. Another similarity between Charlie and David is that they both have two children.

3. However, David has two girls, and Charlie has one girl and one boy.

4. Charlie works in an office. On the other hand, David works as a firefighter.

5. The two brothers have similar tastes in music. They both like jazz.

6. Charlie loves to play golf. In contrast, David does not like golf at all.

7. Finally, a major difference between the brothers is that Charlie makes a lot of money, but David doesn't.

CHAPTER 11

Lincoln and Kennedy: Different Times, Similar Destinies

VOCABULARY PREVIEW Page 82

1. I'll say a few words about Lincoln's and Kennedy's tragic fates.

2. Both Lincoln and Kennedy were assassinated while in office.

3. In spite of his lack of formal education, Lincoln became a well-known lawyer.

4. Books have been written about the strange coincidences in the lives of the two men.

5. Lincoln began his political career in Congress.

6. Lincoln and Kennedy were elected to Congress 100 years apart.

7. At the time Kennedy took office, African Americans were being denied their civil rights.

8. Unrest took the form of civil rights demonstrations.

9. Neither president lived to complete his term in office.

NOTETAKING PREPARATION Page 83

1. Today, I'm going to talk to you about one of America's greatest and most respected presidents—Abraham Lincoln. First, I'm going to talk about his early life and

childhood, growing up as a poor boy in Kentucky. Then, I'll be talking about his family life—his marriage and his children. We'll move on then to discussing his professional career as a lawyer in Illinois. Finally, we'll talk about his presidency—how he became president, what he achieved as president, and how his presidency ended in a tragic assassination.

2. My lecture today will tell the story of the man who became the youngest person elected president in United States history—John F. Kennedy. However, I want to start my lecture, not by talking about Kennedy himself, but his father, who was an extremely important person in his life. I'll then be talking about Kennedy's military career in the U.S. Navy and some of the brave things he did during World War II. When he returned from the war, Kennedy went into politics, so I'll be talking next about his early political career. I'll end, of course, by talking about his presidency and how it ended so suddenly and tragically with his assassination.

1. Kennedy lived in the twentieth century, whereas Lincoln lived in the nineteenth.

2. John F. Kennedy went to Harvard University; in contrast, Lincoln was basically a self-educated man who had very little formal education.

3. Kennedy came from a very wealthy family, while Lincoln grew up in a poor family.

4. It is true that both men were assassinated while they were president; however, Kennedy was assassinated during his first term in office and Lincoln near the beginning of his second.

5. One difference between the two presidents is that they came from different political parties.

FIRST LISTENING   Page 84

Lecturer: In this lecture, I'd like to share some thoughts about two famous Americans, Abraham Lincoln and John F. Kennedy. First, I'll talk about some of the major differences between the two men. Then, I'll tell you about some similarities between Lincoln and Kennedy. In other words, I'll talk a little about their family and educational backgrounds. Then I'll talk a little more about their political lives. And finally, I'll end by saying a few words about their tragic fates. Both Lincoln and Kennedy were assassinated—killed—while in office. I'm old enough to remember the day in 1963 that President Kennedy was shot in Dallas, Texas. It was a pretty sad day. But I don't want to talk about that sad day now.

How were Lincoln and Kennedy different? Let's see. For one thing, they lived in different times and had very different family and educational backgrounds. Kennedy lived in the twentieth century, last century; Lincoln

lived in the nineteenth century. Kennedy was born in 1917, whereas Lincoln was born more than a hundred years earlier, in 1809. As for their family backgrounds, Kennedy came from a rich family, while Lincoln's family was anything but rich. Because Kennedy came from a wealthy family, he was able to attend expensive, private schools. He graduated from Harvard University. On the other hand, Lincoln had only one year of formal education. In spite of his lack of formal education, Lincoln became a well-known lawyer. He taught himself law by reading law books. You might say Lincoln was a self-educated man.

In spite of these differences in Kennedy and Lincoln's backgrounds, some interesting similarities between the two men are evident. In fact, books have been written about the strange coincidences in the lives of these two men. Take, for example, their political careers. Lincoln began his political career in Congress. Similarly, Kennedy also began his political career in Congress. Lincoln was elected to the U.S. House of Representatives in 1847, and Kennedy was elected to the House in 1947. So they were elected to Congress exactly one hundred years apart. Another interesting coincidence is that each man was elected President of the United States in a year ending with the number 60. Lincoln was elected president in 1860, and Kennedy was elected in 1960; furthermore, both men were president during years of civil unrest in the country. Lincoln was president during the American Civil War. At the time Kennedy became president, African Americans were fighting for their civil rights. Unrest took the form of civil rights demonstrations. Times changed, and in just over 50 more years, the United States elected its first African-American president, Barack Obama. President Obama was elected in 2008 and— But let me get back to talking about Lincoln and Kennedy.

Another striking similarity between these two men was that, as you probably know, neither president lived to complete his term in office. Lincoln and Kennedy were both assassinated while in office. Kennedy was assassinated in 1963, in Dallas, Texas, after only 1,000 days in office. Lincoln was assassinated in 1865 a few days after the end of the American Civil War. It is rather curious to note that both presidents were shot while they were sitting next to their wives.

These are only a few examples of the unusual, similarities in the destinies of these two Americans— men who had a tremendous impact on the social and political life of the United States and on the imagination of the American people.

SECOND LISTENING   Page 84

I'd like to share some thoughts about two famous Americans. • I'll talk about the major differences between Abraham Lincoln and John F. Kennedy. • I'll talk about their family and educational backgrounds. • I'll talk about their political lives. • I'll end up saying a few words about their tragic fates. • How were they different? • Kennedy and Lincoln lived in different times. • Kennedy lived in the twentieth century. • Lincoln lived in the nineteenth century • Kennedy was born in 1917. • Lincoln was born in 1809. • Kennedy came from a rich family. • He went to expensive private schools. • He graduated from Harvard University. • Lincoln had only one year of formal education. • He taught himself law and became a lawyer. • He was a self-educated man. • There are interesting similarities in the lives of the two men. • Lincoln began his political career in Congress. • Kennedy began his political career in Congress. • Lincoln was elected to Congress in 1846. • Kennedy was elected to Congress in 1946. • Lincoln was elected president in 1860. • Kennedy was elected president in 1960. • Lincoln and Kennedy were presidents during years of civil unrest. • Lincoln was president during the American Civil War. • During Kennedy's term there were civil rights demonstrations. • Neither lived to complete his term as president. • Lincoln was assassinated in 1865. • Kennedy was assassinated in 1963, in Dallas, Texas. • Both men had a tremendous impact on the social and political life of the United States. • Both had an impact on the imagination of the American people.

THIRD LISTENING Page 84

Part 1

Lecturer: In this lecture, I'd like to share some thoughts about two famous Americans, Abraham Lincoln and John F. Kennedy. First, I'll talk about some of the major differences between the two men. Then, I'll tell you about some similarities between Lincoln and Kennedy. In other words, I'll talk a little about their family and educational backgrounds. Then I'll talk a little more about their political lives. And finally, I'll end by saying a few words about their tragic fates. Both Lincoln and Kennedy were assassinated—killed—while in office. I'm old enough to remember the day in 1963 that President Kennedy was shot in Dallas, Texas. It was a pretty sad day. But I don't want to talk about that sad day now.

How were Lincoln and Kennedy different? Let's see. For one thing, they lived in different times and had very different family and educational backgrounds. Kennedy lived in the twentieth century, last century; Lincoln lived in the nineteenth century. Kennedy was born in 1917, whereas Lincoln was born more than a hundred years earlier, in 1809. As for their family backgrounds, Kennedy came from a rich family, while Lincoln's family was anything but rich. Because Kennedy came from a wealthy family, he was able to attend expensive, private schools. He graduated from Harvard University. On

the other hand, Lincoln had only one year of formal education. In spite of his lack of formal education, Lincoln became a well-known lawyer. He taught himself law by reading law books. You might say Lincoln was a self-educated man.

Part 2

See First Listening, above.

ACCURACY CHECK Page 85

1. In what century was Lincoln born?
2. Why was Kennedy able to attend expensive private schools?
3. How many years did Lincoln attend school?
4. How did Lincoln get most of his education?
5. How did Kennedy and Lincoln begin their political careers?
6. When was Kennedy elected president?
7. During what war was Lincoln president?
8. How did both Kennedy and Lincoln die?
9. How long was Kennedy president of the United States?
10. When was Lincoln murdered?

EXPANSION TASK 1 Page 86

1. Both women were 24 years old when they married.
2. Neither of the women were interested in politics.
3. Another similarity between the women is that they both spoke French.
4. Both Mrs. Lincoln and Mrs. Kennedy suffered the death of a child while First Lady.
5. Neither Mrs. Kennedy nor Mrs. Lincoln was injured by her husband's assassin.

EXPANSION TASK 2 Page 87

1. The first obvious similarity is that the last name of both vice presidents was *Johnson*.
2. Both Andrew Johnson and Lyndon Johnson were large, tall men.
3. Neither of the vice presidents was from the north.
4. Both men became president following the assassination of the president of the United States.
5. Lyndon Johnson was later elected president of the United States, whereas Andrew Johnson was not.
6. Andrew Johnson had 13 letters in his name, and Lyndon Johnson did, also.
7. Kennedy's vice president was born at the beginning of the twentieth century. On the other hand, Lincoln's

vice president was born at the beginning of the nineteenth century.

See A, above.

CHAPTER 12

The *Titanic* and the *Costa Concordia*: Tragedies at Sea

VOCABULARY PREVIEW Page 89

1. On the morning of April 10, 1912, the *Titanic* set sail from England.
2. Reports of the sinking—or the partial sinking—of the *Costa Concordia* filled the newspapers, television, and the Internet for days.
3. As each ship was sinking, there were acts of courage.
4. Some men on the *Titanic* gave up their seats in the lifeboats to women and children.
5. So, on the *Costa Concordia*, there were also acts of courage and acts of cowardice.
6. I'd like to point out some of the big differences between these two ship disasters.
7. Another difference was what caused these ships to sink.
8. The *Titanic* struck an iceberg.
9. The *Costa Concordia* struck a shelf of rocks near an island.

NOTETAKING PREPARATION Page 90

Alicia: Carlos, can you help me? I missed a part of the lecture on the sinking of the *Titanic* and the *Costa Concordia*.

Carlos: Sure, Alicia, I'll help you if I can. What did you miss?

Alicia: Well, first of all the lecturer said there were acts of courage, but also acts of *cow*-something. What was that word?

Carlos: Cowardice? You know, when people are not brave. They're cowards.

Alicia: Oh. OK. Thanks. I see, so the captain of the *Costa Concordia* was a coward when he left the ship? So how did he leave the ship? I didn't understand that.

Carlos: OK. Let me look at my notes. Oh yes, apparently the captain said he tripped in the dark and fell into a lifeboat and that is how he left the ship. I guess he was saying it was a mistake.

Alicia: Oh. OK. I get it. Let me write that in my notes. And so the captain of the *Titanic*, then, stayed on the ship and drowned. And what happened to the captain of the *Costa Concordia*?

Carlos: He survived.

Alicia: Oh, right. Let me write that in my notes, too. Hey, listen Carlos, thanks so much for your help.

Carlos: No problem. Actually, Alicia, there was a part of the lecture I didn't get. Can you . . .

1. Both the *Titanic* and the *Concordia* were enormous luxury ships.
2. The *Titanic* struck an iceberg, while the *Costa Concordia* struck rocks.
3. Another similarity is that as each ship was sinking there were acts of great courage.
4. There were not enough lifeboats on the *Titanic*. In contrast, there were plenty of lifeboats on the *Costa Concordia*.
5. People lost their lives on the *Concordia*; however, there was much greater loss of life on the *Titanic*.

FIRST LISTENING Page 91

Lecturer: On the morning of April 10, 1912, the *Titanic* set sail from England. Four days later, she lay at the bottom of the Atlantic Ocean.

On the evening of January 13, 2012, the *Costa Concordia* set sail from Italy. A day later, the ship lay partly sunk off the coast of Italy.

Reports of the sinking—or the partial sinking—of the *Costa Concordia* filled the newspapers, television, and the Internet for days. Almost immediately, people began to compare the sinking of the *Concordia* with the sinking of the *Titanic*. There were a number of unusual similarities between the two events. However, there were also some major differences. I'll focus my talk today on pointing out some of those similarities and differences.

OK, what are some of the similarities between these two ships? Well, first of all, both the *Titanic* and the *Costa Concordia* were enormous. In fact, the *Titanic* was the largest ship of her day. She was 882 feet long with 9 decks. The *Costa Concordia* was a little larger than the *Titanic* at 951 feet long with 13 passenger decks. So, both were, indeed, megaships of their time. Today, even larger passenger ships are sailing the seas—ships that are longer and higher and heavier, but that's a topic for another day. Where was I? OK. So both ships were megaships of their time. Also, both the *Titanic* and the *Costa Concordia* were luxury ships, with pools, restaurants, a variety of activities, and places for the passengers to relax and enjoy their time on board.

Let's see. Another similarity is that as each ship was sinking there were acts of courage. And, there were also acts of cowardice. Yes, the way some people acted was very brave. For example, a number of the men on board the *Titanic* gave up their seats in the lifeboats to women and children. The rule on the *Titanic* as it was sinking was "Women and children first." At the same time, there were some on the *Titanic* who acted like cowards. One man, for example, dressed as a woman so he could get into a lifeboat and save his own life.

OK. So, on the *Costa Concordia* there were also acts of courage and acts of cowardice. At times aboard the sinking *Costa Concordia* it seemed to be "Every man for himself." In fact, the captain of the *Concordia* left his ship before all the passengers and crew were safely off. It's rather strange. The captain said he tripped in the dark and fell into a lifeboat. The Italian Coast Guard ordered him to return to his ship, but he refused to go back.

Many people today still think the captain should be the last person to leave a sinking ship. As you probably know, the captain of the *Titanic* went down with his ship. The captain of the *Costa Concordia* left his ship and survived.

All right. Now I'd like to spend a few minutes pointing out some of the big differences between these two ship disasters. Oh! I guess I already touched on one difference—the fate of the two captains. So, let me continue. The *Titanic* was a transatlantic ocean liner, that is, a ship that provided transportation across the Atlantic Ocean. She—or it—sank in the deep, cold, ocean waters. The *Costa Concordia* was a cruise ship that provided vacation tours around the Mediterranean Sea. The *Concordia* sank in warmer, shallow water near the coast. She—it—came to rest on its, er . . . her side with much of the ship above the water.

Another difference between the two events is what caused these ships to sink. The *Titanic* struck an iceberg, while in contrast, the *Costa Concordia* struck a shelf of rocks near an island off the Italian coast. So, although the ships sank for a similar reason—they struck something under water—they each struck something quite different: the *Titanic*, an iceberg; the *Costa Concordia*, rocks.

But, of course, the greatest difference between these two terrible accidents was the number of lives lost. When the *Titanic* sank, more than 1,500 people died. They drowned or froze to death in the icy North Atlantic water. A few more then 700 people survived the sinking of the *Titanic*. In the *Costa Concordia* accident, 32 people lost their lives. Two remained missing. Almost 4,200 people survived the disaster.

One of the reasons that so many people on the *Titanic* died was that the ship carried only about half the number of lifeboats needed to rescue all the people on the ship. And most of those lifeboats weren't full when they left the *Titanic*. Many people never had a chance to be saved. In contrast, the *Concordia* had extra lifeboats, with room for 25 percent more people than the ship could hold. But, because the ship was lying on its side, many of the lifeboats couldn't be lowered into the water.

Oh, by the way, did you ever see the movie *Titanic*? With Leonardo DiCaprio and Kate Winslet. If you haven't seen it, I highly recommend it. And speaking of the movie, a Swiss tourist aboard the *Costa Concordia* reported that the song from the movie, "My Heart Will Go On," was playing in the dining room when the sound of the crash was heard by the diners. Isn't that . . . strange? Why would they play that song on a ship!

All right, let me end by noting that whenever people travel for business or adventure on ships, trains, or planes, the possibility of disaster is always present. Most people arrive safely at their destination, but accidents like shipwrecks and train wrecks and plane crashes do happen. The *Titanic* and the *Costa Concordia* remind us that no matter how safe we are told to feel, accidents can happen suddenly and unexpectedly. You need to be on your toes when something happens. Remember, the vast majority of people do arrive safely at their destinations whether they take a ship, plane, train, or, for that matter, a car. But not always! Well, that's it for today.

SECOND LISTENING Page 91

On April 10, 1912, the *Titanic* set sail from England. • Four days later, she lay at the bottom of the Atlantic Ocean. • On January 13, 2012, the *Costa Concordia* set sail from Italy. • A day later, the ship lay partly sunk off the coast of Italy. • People compared the sinking of the *Concordia* with the sinking of the *Titanic*. • There were a number of unusual similarities between the two events. • However, there were also some major differences. • I'll point out some of those similarities and differences. • What are some of the similarities between these two ships? • Both the *Titanic* and the *Costa Concordia* were enormous. • The *Titanic* was the largest ship of her day. • She was 882 feet long with 9 decks. • The *Costa Concordia* was 951 feet long with 13 passenger decks. • Both ships were megaships of their time. • Both the *Titanic* and the *Costa Concordia* were luxury ships. • As each ship was sinking, there were acts of courage. • And, there were also acts of cowardice. • Yes, the way some people acted was very brave. • For example, some men on board the *Titanic* gave up their seats in the lifeboats. • They gave up their seats in the lifeboats to women and children. • The rule was "Women and children first." • But some on the *Titanic* acted like cowards. • For example, one man dressed as a woman so he could get into a lifeboat. • On the *Costa Concordia* there were also acts of courage and of cowardice. • At times it seemed to be "Every man for himself." • The captain of the *Concordia* left his ship before all the passengers and crew were safe. • He tripped in the dark and fell into a lifeboat. • The Italian Coast Guard ordered the captain to return to his ship. • But he refused to go back. • Many people today still think the captain should be the last person to leave a sinking ship. • The captain of the *Titanic* went down with his ship. • The captain of the *Costa Concordia* left his ship and survived. • What were some of the big differences between these two ship disasters? • I already touched on one difference—the fate of the two captains. • The *Titanic* was a transatlantic ocean liner. • It was a ship that provided transportation across the Atlantic Ocean. • The *Titanic* sank in the deep, cold, ocean waters. • The *Costa Concordia* was a cruise ship. • It provided vacation tours around the Mediterranean Sea. • The *Concordia* sank in warmer, shallow water near the coast. • She came to rest on her side with much of the ship above the water. • Another difference between the two events is what caused these ships to sink. • The *Titanic* struck an iceberg. • The *Costa Concordia* struck a shelf of rocks near an island off the Italian coast. • The ships sank for a similar *reason*, but they each struck something *different*—the *Titanic*, an iceberg; the *Costa Concordia*, rocks. • The greatest difference between these two accidents was the number of lives lost. • When the *Titanic* sank, more than 1,500 people died. • A few more than 700 people survived the sinking of the Titanic. • In the *Costa Concordia* accident, 32 people lost their lives. • Almost 4,200 people survived the disaster. • The *Titanic* carried about half the number of lifeboats needed for all the people. • And most of those lifeboats weren't full when they left the *Titanic*. • Many people never had a chance to be saved. • The *Concordia* had lifeboats for more people than the ship could hold. • But, because the ship was on its side, many lifeboats couldn't be lowered into the water. • Whenever people travel, the possibility of disaster is present. • Accidents like shipwrecks and train wrecks and plane crashes do happen. • No matter how safe we are told to feel, accidents can happen suddenly and unexpectedly. • You need to be on your toes when something happens. • The vast majority of people arrive safely at their destinations. • But not always!

THIRD LISTENING   Page 91
Page 91

Part 1

Lecturer: On the morning of April 10, 1912, the *Titanic* set sail from England. Four days later, she lay at the bottom of the Atlantic Ocean.

On the evening of January 13, 2012, the *Costa Concordia* set sail from Italy. A day later, the ship lay partly sunk off the coast of Italy.

Reports of the sinking—or the partial sinking—of the *Costa Concordia* filled the newspapers, television,

and the Internet for days. Almost immediately, people began to compare the sinking of the *Concordia* with the sinking of the *Titanic*. There were a number of unusual similarities between the two events. However, there were also some major differences. I'll focus my talk today on pointing out some of those similarities and differences.

OK, what are some of the similarities between these two ships? Well, first of all, both the *Titanic* and the *Costa Concordia* were enormous. In fact, the *Titanic* was the largest ship of her day. She was 882 feet long with 9 decks. The *Costa Concordia* was a little larger than the *Titanic* at 951 feet long with 13 passenger decks. So, both were, indeed, megaships of their time. Today, even larger passenger ships are sailing the seas—ships that are longer and higher and heavier, but that's a topic for another day. Where was I? OK. So both ships were megaships of their time. Also, both the *Titanic* and the *Costa Concordia* were luxury ships, with pools, restaurants, a variety of activities, and places for the passengers to relax and enjoy their time on board.

Let's see. Another similarity is that as each ship was sinking there were acts of courage. And, there were also acts of cowardice. Yes, the way some people acted was very brave. For example, a number of the men on board the *Titanic* gave up their seats in the lifeboats to women and children. The rule on the *Titanic* as it was sinking was, "Women and children first." At the same time, there were some on the *Titanic* who acted like cowards. One man, for example, dressed as a woman so he could get into a lifeboat and save his own life.

Part 2

See First Listening, above.

ACCURACY CHECK   Page 92
Page 92

1. When did the *Costa Concordia* set sail from Italy?
2. From what country did the *Titanic* set sail?
3. How were the *Titanic* and the *Costa Concordia* similar in size?
4. Which statement is true?
5. Which ship had 13 passenger decks?
6. How many people aboard the *Costa Concordia* died?
7. How was the *Titanic*'s sinking different from the *Costa Concordia*'s?
8. What is true about traveling in ships?

1. The *Titanic* set sail from England and the *Costa Concordia* set sail from Italy.
2. The *Titanic* was a luxury ship, as was the *Costa Concordia*.
3. Both ships struck something under water.

4. The captain of the *Titanic* went down with his ship, but the captain of the *Costa Concordia* left the ship as it was sinking.

5. Most people were rescued from the *Costa Concordia*, while few were rescued from the *Titanic*.

6. The *Titanic* did not safely complete its journey, and neither did the *Costa Concordia*.

EXPANSION TASK 1   Page 93

1. The *Hindenburg* and the *Titanic* were both luxury passenger ships. The difference was that one of them was an airship and the other was an ocean liner.

2. Both vessels created a lot of excitement among the general public. They both represented the beginning of a new era of luxury travel.

3. The *Titanic* sank on its maiden voyage after hitting an iceberg. The *Hindenburg*, on the other hand, caught fire and crashed on its second voyage.

4. Like the *Titanic*, there were survivors from the *Hindenburg* crash. Of the 97 people on board the *Hindenburg*, 35 people died and 62 survived.

5. No news crews witnessed the sinking of the *Titanic*. However, the crash of the *Hindenburg* was filmed. One reporter, Herbert Morrison, gave a breathless account that millions listened to on the radio.

EXPANSION TASK 2   Page 93

1. There are some people who have many friends and everybody likes them. The word for these people is *popular*. On the other hand, there are people who are known by a lot of people, perhaps because they are on television or are often in the news. These people are "well-known." Not all people who are well-known are popular. And people who are popular are not usually well-known. You, for example, may be popular, but not well-known.

2. If a person is not just well-known but very well-known, we call that person *famous*. Now, there is another word in English that is similar to *famous*. It is spelled the same as famous, but with the prefix "in" in front of it. That word is pronounced *infamous*. Now, you might think that infamous means the opposite of famous, but that is not the case. An infamous person is also famous or well-known, but their fame is because of something bad that they have done.

3. People who are not popular may have no friends and feel bad about it. We call these people *lonely*. They are unhappy because they have no friends or are not with their friends. A word that is similar to *lonely* but does not mean the same thing is *alone*. When a person is alone, it means that there are no other people with them or near them. You can be alone in the street, for example, when no one else is there. That doesn't mean you are lonely.

4. An easily confused pair is *a few* and *few*. Many students of English think that *a few* and *few* are similar in meaning, but they are not. *Few* means almost none. So if you say, "Few people in the room were millionaires," it means almost nobody in the room was a millionaire. But if you say, "A few people in the room were millionaires," it means not many, but perhaps more than you would think. So when we use *a few*, we mean a small, but positive number, and when we use *few*, we mean a small number and we are stressing how small the number is.

UNIT 5

Cause and Effect

  CHAPTER 13

Dinosaurs: Why They Disappeared

VOCABULARY PREVIEW   Page 99

A

1. Scientists suggest several theories for why dinosaurs became extinct.

2. Perhaps one day we will know for certain why dinosaurs such as the *Tyrannosaurus rex* died out.

3. We continue to speculate and to search for why dinosaurs disappeared.

4. The change in climate caused a severe shortage of food.

5. Many scientists believe that gradual climate change best explains why the dinosaurs disappeared.

6. The second theory suggests that a huge asteroid hit the earth about 65 million years ago, when the dinosaurs still ruled the earth.

7. The enormous dust cloud covered the whole earth and blocked out the sun for months and months.

8. Iridium is an element that is not common on earth.

9. Today scientists continue to debate these two theories and others, too.

NOTETAKING PREPARATION   Page 100

A

1. Dinosaurs became extinct because the planet's climate changed.

2. The climate of the world became cooler. As a result, plants began to disappear.

3. When the asteroid hit the earth, it caused a huge cloud of dust.

4. Their food vanished, therefore, the dinosaurs vanished, too.

5. Perhaps they'll find out that dinosaurs died out as a result of disease.

See A, above.

FIRST LISTENING Page 101

Lecturer: I'd like to start today's lecture with a question or two: What happened to the dinosaurs? Why did the dinosaurs of 65 million years ago disappear? Any ideas?

Well, no one knows for sure, and the cause of the dinosaurs' disappearance remains a mystery. However, scientists have suggested a number of theories for why dinosaurs became extinct. These theories include the gradual climate-change theory and the asteroid impact theory. I'm going to spend some time talking about these two theories. There are a number of other theories, but the climate change and asteroid theories are among the most talked about today. Perhaps one day we will know for certain why dinosaurs such as the *Tyrannosaurus rex* died out. But until that day, we will continue to speculate and continue to search for answers to why these creatures disappeared.

So, let me talk about the climate change theory first. This theory suggests that dinosaurs became extinct because the planet's climate changed. It says that over millions of years the world gradually became cooler. By the way, many scientists think that climate change is happening even today, but they think the climate is getting hotter rather than colder. But, that's a topic for another day. Let me return to the disappearance of the dinosaurs.

So, some scientists speculate that in the time of the dinosaurs, the climate of the world gradually changed and became cooler. As a result, the plants that the dinosaurs usually ate began to disappear. The change in climate caused a severe shortage of food for the dinosaurs, since most dinosaurs were plant eaters. In other words, dinosaurs were vegetarians, and the types of plants they depended on for their food supply were disappearing. So, according to the theory of gradual climate change, the cause of the disappearance of the dinosaurs was a change in climate that changed the type of plants available for food.

Many scientists, but by no means all scientists, believe that gradual climate change best explains why the dinosaurs disappeared. Many other scientists think the dinosaurs may not have disappeared gradually and slowly over centuries. They speculate that the dinosaurs disappeared quickly and suddenly.

This brings us to the asteroid impact theory. This theory suggests that a huge asteroid hit the earth about 65 million years ago, when the dinosaurs still walked the earth. When this asteroid hit the earth, it caused a huge cloud of dust. The enormous dust cloud covered the whole earth and blocked out the sun for months and months. Since there was no sun for many months, most of the plants on earth died. The dinosaurs' food supply disappeared in a period of months.

Until a few decades ago there was little evidence that an asteroid or a comet *had* hit the earth 65 million years ago. However, in the late twentieth century scientists found large amounts of an element called "iridium." This iridium is in layers of earth that are 65 million years old. In other words, the iridium is in the same earth and rock layers as many of the bones of the last dinosaurs. This element is not common on earth. It exists deep within the earth, but it is unusual to find iridium near the earth's surface. However, there is a lot of iridium in space. Scientists speculate that iridium arrived on earth 65 million years ago when a comet or asteroid hit the earth.

The asteroid impact theory explains two things. For one thing, it explains the larger amounts of the rare element iridium that is in the 65-million-year-old layers of earth and rock, and for another, it explains why the dinosaurs disappeared: Their food vanished, therefore, the dinosaurs vanished, too.

Today scientists continue to debate these two theories and others, too. In the future, scientists may find evidence that supports a totally new theory of why the dinosaurs died out. Perhaps they'll find out that dinosaurs died out as a result of disease. But we'll have to wait for further evidence and future research. Well, that's about it for today. Thank you, everyone.

SECOND LISTENING Page 101

I'd like to start today's lecture with a question or two. • What happened to the dinosaurs? • Why did the dinosaurs of 65 million years ago disappear? • The cause of their disappearance remains a mystery. • However, a number of theories have been proposed. • These theories include the gradual climate-change theory and the asteroid impact theory. • There are a number of other theories. • But the climate change and the asteroid theories are among the most talked about today. • Perhaps one day we will know for certain why dinosaurs like the *Tyrannosaurus rex* died out. • We will continue to speculate why these creatures became extinct. • Let me talk about the climate change theory first. • This theory suggests that dinosaurs became extinct because the planet's climate changed. • Over millions of years the world gradually became cooler. • Scientists speculate the climate of the world gradually changed and became cooler. • As a result, the plants the dinosaurs usually ate began to disappear. • The change in climate caused a severe shortage of food for the dinosaurs, • Most dinosaurs were plant eaters. • They were vegetarians. • The plants they depended on for their food supply were disappearing. • The disappearance of the dinosaurs was caused directly by a shortage of plants to eat. • The disappearance of the dinosaurs was caused indirectly by the change in climate. • Many scientists believe that gradual climate change is why the dinosaurs disappeared. • Many other scientists think the dinosaurs may not have disappeared gradually and slowly. • They speculate that the dinosaurs disappeared quickly and suddenly. • The asteroid impact theory suggests that an asteroid hit the earth 65 million years ago. • When this asteroid hit the earth, it caused a huge cloud of dust. • The dust cloud covered the whole earth and blocked out the sun for months. • Since there was no sun for many months, most of the plants on earth died. • The dinosaur's food supply was destroyed in a period of months. • Until a few decades ago there was little evidence that an asteroid *had* hit the earth. • In the late twentieth century scientists found iridium all over the world. • This iridium was found in layers of earth that are 65 million years old. • The iridium was found in the layers of earth where the bones of the last dinosaurs were found. • This element is not common on earth. • It exists deep within the earth. • It is not common to find iridium near the earth's surface. • Iridium is an element that is often found in space. • Scientists speculate that iridium was brought to earth when a comet or asteroid hit the earth. • The asteroid impact theory explains two things about the reason dinosaurs disappeared. • It explains the larger amounts of iridium found in the 65-million-year-old layers of earth. • The asteroid impact explains why the dinosaurs disappeared from the earth. • Their food vanished, therefore, the dinosaurs vanished, too. • Today scientists continue to debate these two theories and others, too. • In the future evidence may be found that supports a totally new theory. • A new theory of why the dinosaurs died out. • Perhaps they'll find out that dinosaurs died out as a result of disease. • We'll have to wait for further evidence and future research.

THIRD LISTENING Page 101

Part 1

Lecturer: I'd like to start today's lecture with a question or two: What happened to the dinosaurs? Why did the dinosaurs of 65 million years ago disappear? Any ideas?

Well, no one knows for sure, and the cause of the dinosaurs' disappearance remains a mystery. However, scientists have suggested a number of theories for why dinosaurs became extinct. These theories include the

gradual climate change theory and the asteroid impact theory. I'm going to spend some time talking about these two theories. There are a number of other theories, but the climate change and asteroid theories are among the most talked about today. Perhaps one day we will know for certain why dinosaurs such as the *Tyrannosaurus rex* died out. But until that day, we will continue to speculate and continue to search for answers to why these creatures became extinct.

So, let me talk about the climate change theory first. This theory suggests that dinosaurs became extinct because the planet's climate changed. It says that over millions of years the world gradually became cooler. By the way, many scientists think that climate change is happening even today, but they think the climate is getting hotter rather than colder. But, that's a topic for another day. Let me return to the disappearance of the dinosaurs.

So, some scientists speculate that in the time of the dinosaurs, the climate of the world gradually changed and became cooler. As a result, the plants that the dinosaurs usually ate began to disappear. The change in climate caused a severe shortage of food for the dinosaurs, since most dinosaurs were plant eaters. In other words, dinosaurs were vegetarians, and the types of plants they depended on for their food supply were disappearing. So, according to the theory of gradual climate change, the cause of the disappearance of the dinosaurs was a change in climate that changed type of plants available for food.

Part 2

See First Listening, above.

ACCURACY CHECK Page 102

1. One of the two theories of why the dinosaurs disappeared is called the asteroid impact theory. What is the other theory?

2. For about how long was the climate of the earth becoming colder at the time the dinosaurs roamed the earth?

3. When the climate gradually became cooler during the age of the dinosaurs, what happened to their food source?

4. What happened when (and if) an asteroid or comet hit the earth at the time when the dinosaurs lived?

5. Why was it surprising that iridium was found in the rock layers where the bones of dinosaurs are located?

1. According to the climate change theory, a cloud of dust blocked out the sun.

2. The two theories discussed in the lecture are the only theories possible.

3. The element iridium is commonly found on earth.

4. The lecturer mentioned the *Tyrannosaurus rex* as an example of the kind of dinosaurs that existed long ago.

5. In the future, a new theory of why the dinosaurs disappeared may be developed.

EXPANSION TASK 1 Page 103

1. My television set isn't working. What is wrong with it?

2. Lin doesn't want to go to the picnic today. Why doesn't she want to go?

3. Henry was fired from his job at the bank. Why did he lose his job?

4. John was born in Paris, France, in 1975. Why was he born in Paris?

5. All of the students in the class passed the examination except Antonia. Why didn't she pass?

6. You are trying to call your doctor, but nobody answers the phone. What's the reason there's no answer?

7. Tony lost a lot of money gambling in Monte Carlo. Why?

8. Hamid is wearing tennis clothes and carrying a tennis racket. Why is he dressed in those clothes?

EXPANSION TASK 2 Page 104

1. It's a cold and snowy night. A man and a woman are traveling in a car. They are driving along a mountain road. It is difficult to see out the car's windshield because the snow is falling so hard and because one of the windshield wipers is broken. Suddenly, there is a sharp curve in the road. The man steps on the brakes hard. What happens?

2. It's the second half of a championship soccer game. Both teams have scored three goals. The score is 3–3. Suddenly the forward on one of the teams gets the ball. He takes it toward the goal. He's close to the goal. He kicks the ball. What happens?

3. A fisherman is walking by the side of the river. Suddenly he hears a young boy calling for help. The man looks toward the river and sees the boy. The boy is trying to stay on top of the water. The man is not a good swimmer. What happens?

4. You and your friend are sitting in the movie theater watching a movie. A man walks into your row. He is looking for a seat. He is carrying popcorn. Some of it goes on your friend's head. People behind you are

angry. You are angry. Your friend gets up to talk to the man. What happens?

5. A man is crossing a street in New York. A policeman watches him carefully. The policeman sees something in the man's left hand. He wants to talk to the man. He comes up to him. What happens?

CHAPTER 14

The U.S. Civil War: Why It Happened

VOCABULARY PREVIEW Page 106

1. I'm a descendant of a soldier who fought for the Union—that is, the North—in the Civil War.

2. There were a number of reasons for tension between the North and the South.

3. Slavery was, in fact, the foundation of the economy in the South.

4. In the South there were large plantations that grew cotton and tobacco.

5. Many Southerners feared that the North would dominate the country.

6. When Abraham Lincoln became President of the United States, the South decided it was time to secede from the Union.

7. The people of the South were afraid that their way of life was in danger.

8. The Civil War led to the devastation of the South.

9. The South today is a vital part of these United States.

NOTETAKING PREPARATION Page 107

1. A colleague of mine from Georgia once referred to it as the War of Northern Aggression. I'm a descendant of a soldier who fought for the Union—that is, the North—in the Civil War, and was very surprised by that name.

2. American historian Drew Gilpin Faust notes that the number of Northern and Southern soldiers who died between 1861 and 1865 was equal to 2 percent of the population.

3. As I said, there were a number of reasons for tension between the North and the South before the war began. One of these was *the tension between the North and the South over the issue of slavery.*

4. As a result, many Southerners began to fear that the North would dominate the country both economically and politically. Because of this fear, many Southerners believed that the South should secede.

5. Abraham Lincoln was against the spread of slavery into new states. Because of this, the people of the South were afraid that their way of life was in danger with Lincoln as president.

6. I'd like to finish up by noting that the South today is an essential part—no, a vital part—of these United States of America.

1. What caused this terrible war between the North and the South?

2. As I said, there were a number of reasons for tension between the North and the South.

3. This tension was one that eventually led to war.

4. Industry brought wealth to the North. As a result, Southerners began to fear that the North would dominate the country.

5. Many historians believe the North won the war mainly because of its economic strength.

6. The Civil War had three important results for the United States.

FIRST LISTENING   Page 108

Lecturer: Today, I'm going spend some time exploring the causes and effects of an important event in American history, the U.S. Civil War, or as it is sometimes called, the War between the States. This was a war between the states in the northern part and the states in the southern part of the United States of America.

You know, some people have referred to the Civil War as the War of Rebellion or the Brothers' War. A colleague of mine from Georgia once referred to it as the War of Northern Aggression. I'm a descendant of a soldier who fought for the Union—that is, the North—in the Civil War, and was very surprised by that name.

OK. So the U.S. Civil War was fought more than 150 years ago. It began in 1861 and lasted until 1865. The battles fought in the U.S. Civil War resulted in the deaths of over 620,000 soldiers. In fact, American historian Drew Gilpin Faust notes that the number of Northern and Southern soldiers who died between 1861 and 1865 was equal to 2 percent of the population. The soldiers died of disease as well as battle injuries. Oh, another point: tens of thousands of civilians also died in the war, particularly in the South, where most of the fighting took place.

What caused this terrible war between the North and the South in the United States? Well, many of the causes resulted from the tension that existed between the northern and the southern regions of the country from the very beginning of the United States. I'll talk about three reasons for this tension, or what historians call three *causes* of the War between the States.

As I said, there were a number of reasons for tension between the North and the South before the war began. One of these was *the tension between the North and the South over the issue of slavery.*

The Southern way of life and the Southern economy at that time were based on the use of slave labor. For almost 250 years before the Civil War began, the economy of the South depended on the labor of slaves. The slaves were used to plant and pick cotton and tobacco. Cotton and tobacco were the main crops grown in the South. Most Southerners did *not* own slaves. But the majority of Southerners did not think it was wrong to own, buy, or sell slaves. Slavery was, in fact, the foundation of the economy in the South.

This was not the same in the North because the Northern economy did not depend this way on the use of slave labor. Why not? Well, for one thing, in the South there were many large plantations that grew cotton and tobacco. In the North, however, there were small farms. The Northern farmers planted many different kinds of crops. They did not depend on single large crops of a product like cotton or tobacco. The Northern farmers did not need many slaves, since most of their farms were smaller than most of the Southern plantations. Many Northerners were opposed to slavery. And, many people wanted to keep slavery out of any new states that would join the Union in future years. In fact, many Northerners wanted to end slavery completely.

This attitude against slavery made many Southerners angry. So, for many years before the war, there was this constant tension between the North and the South over the issue of slavery. This tension was one that eventually led to war.

Another tension between the North and the South resulted from *the growth of industry in the North.*

While the South remained agricultural in the nineteenth century, the North became more and more industrial. As industry increased in the North, it brought more people and greater wealth to the northern states. As a result, many Southerners began to fear that the North would dominate the country both economically and politically. Because of this fear, many Southerners believed that the South should secede—leave the Union—and it should form its own country. The North opposed the idea of the South leaving the Union.

In 1860, when Abraham Lincoln became president, the South decided it was time to secede from the Union. As you probably know, Abraham Lincoln was against the spread of slavery into new states. Because of this, the people of the South were afraid that their way of life was in danger with Lincoln as president.

As a result, the *tension that was caused by the election of Abraham Lincoln* was a third major cause of the Civil War.

After four years of terrible fighting, the North won the war with the South, and the United States remained one country. Many historians believe the North won the war mainly because of its economic strength and its industrial power.

In the end, the Civil War had three important results for the United States: (1) the Civil War kept the United States together as *one* country; (2) the Civil War led to the end of slavery in the United States; and (3) the Civil War led to the devastation of the South and the destruction of the plantations its economy had been based on.

I'd like to finish up by noting that the South today is an essential part—no, a vital part—of these United States of America. Well, that's all the time we have for now. See you next time.

SECOND LISTENING Page 108

Today, I'm going to be talking about the causes and effects of the U.S. Civil War. • It is sometimes called the War between the States. • It was a war between the states in the Northern and Southern part of the United States. • Some people have referred to the Civil War as the War of Rebellion or the Brothers' War. • A colleague from Georgia referred to the Civil War as the War of Northern Aggression. • I was very surprised by that name. • The U.S. Civil War was fought more than 150 years ago. • It began in 1861 and lasted until 1865. • The battles fought resulted in the deaths of over 620,000 soldiers alone. • The number of Northern and Southern soldiers killed would equal 6 million soldiers today. • Many soldiers died of disease and battle wounds. • Tens of thousands also died, particularly in the South. • The battles of the war were fought mostly in the backyards, farms, and cities of the South. • What caused this terrible civil war between the North and the South? • There was tension between the northern and southern regions from the very beginning. • There were three reasons for this tension, or three *causes* of the War between the States. • There were reasons for tension between the North and the South before the war began. • There was tension between the North and the South over the issue of slavery. • The Southern way of life and economy were based on the use of slave labor. • For 250 years the economy of the South depended on the labor of slaves. • The slaves planted and picked cotton and tobacco, the main crops grown in the South. • Most Southerners did *not* own slaves. • But the majority of Southerners did not think it was wrong to own, buy, or sell slaves. • Slavery was the foundation of the economy in the South. • The Northern economy did not depend on the use of slave labor. • Why not? • In the South there were many large plantations that grew cotton and tobacco. • In the North, however, there were smaller farms. • The Northern farmers planted many different kinds of crops. • They did not depend on single large crops of a product like cotton or tobacco. • The Northern farmers did not need many slaves. • Most of their Northern farms were smaller than the Southern plantations. • Many Northerners were opposed to slavery. • Many Northerners wanted to keep slavery out of new states joining the Union. • Many Northerners wanted to end slavery completely. • The Northern attitude against slavery made many Southerners angry. • For many years before the war, there was constant tension over the issue of slavery. • This tension eventually led to war. • Another tension involved the growth of industry in the North. • While the South remained agricultural, the North became more and more industrial. • Industry brought more people and greater wealth to the Northern states. • Many Southerners feared the North would dominate economically and politically. • Many Southerners believed that the South should secede from the Union. • Many Southerners believed the South should form its own country. • The North opposed the idea of the South leaving the Union. • In 1860 Abraham Lincoln became president of the United States. • When Lincoln became president, the South decided to secede from the Union. • Abraham Lincoln was against the spread of slavery into new states of the Union. • The people of the South were afraid their way of life was in danger with Lincoln as president. • The tension caused by the election of Abraham Lincoln was a third major cause of the war. • After four years of terrible fighting, the North won the war. • The United States remained one country. • Many historians believe the North won the war with its economic strength and industrial power. • The Civil War had three important results for the United States. • The U.S. Civil War preserved the United States as *one* country. • It led to the end of slavery in the United States. • It led to the devastation of the South. • And it led to the destruction of the plantations the South's economy had been based on. • The South today is an essential part—no, a vital part—of these United States of America.

THIRD LISTENING Page 108

Part 1

Lecturer: Today, I'm going spend some time exploring the causes and effects of an important event in American history, the U.S. Civil War, or as it is sometimes called, the War between the States. This was a war between the states in the northern part and the states in the southern part of the United States of America.

You know, some people have referred to the Civil War as the War of Rebellion or the Brothers' War. A colleague of mine from Georgia once referred to it as the War of Northern Aggression. I'm a descendant of a soldier who fought for the Union—that is, the North—in the Civil War, and was very surprised by that name.

OK. So the U.S. Civil War was fought more than 150 years ago. It began in 1861 and lasted until 1865. The battles fought in the U.S. Civil War resulted in the death of over 620,000 soldiers. In fact, American historian Drew Gilpin Faust notes that the number of Northern and Southern soldiers who died between 1861 and 1865 was equal to 2 percent of the population. The soldiers died of disease as well as battle injuries. Oh, another point: tens of thousands of civilians also died in the war, particularly in the South where most of the fighting took place.

What caused this terrible war between the North and the South of the United States? Well, many of the causes resulted from the tension that existed between the northern and the southern regions of the country from the very beginning of the United States. I'll talk about three reasons for this tension, or what historians call three *causes* of the War between the States.

As I said, there were a number of reasons for tension between the North and the South before the war began. One of these was *the tension between the North and the South over the issue of slavery.*

The Southern way of life and the Southern economy at that time were based on the use of slave labor. For almost 250 years before the Civil War began, the economy of the South depended on the labor of slaves. The slaves were used to plant and pick cotton and tobacco. Cotton and tobacco were the main crops grown in the South. Most Southerners did *not* own slaves. But the majority of Southerners did not think it was wrong to own, buy, or sell slaves. Slavery was, in fact, the foundation of the economy in the South.

`Part 2`

See First Listening, above.

ACCURACY CHECK   Page 109

1. For how long did the economy of the South depend on slavery before the Civil War began?
2. Name one cause of the U.S. Civil War.
3. Why didn't the economy in the North depend on the use of slaves?
4. What was one main reason that the North won the war with the South?

1. Many battles were fought. As a result, many soldiers were killed in the battles. Which was the cause?
2. The tensions between the North and the South were many. Because of that, the Civil War began. Which was the effect?

3. Abraham Lincoln was against the spread of slavery. This idea made many Southerners angry. Which was the cause?
4. Many of the farms in the North were small. Consequently, fewer people were needed to work on the farms. Which was the cause?
5. The North was opposed to the South becoming a separate country. The Civil War was fought to maintain the Union. Which was the effect?

EXPANSION TASK 1   Page 110

1. The American Revolution started because the colonists wanted to have some form of self-government.
2. The British were at a disadvantage during the war on account of the fact that they were fighting a war far from their home country.
3. Since the colonists had fewer weapons and soldiers than the British, at times the colonists used some guerilla warfare tactics.
4. One reason that the colonists won the war was because the French entered the war on their side.

EXPANSION TASK 2   Page 110

1. A man and woman are sitting at a table in a restaurant. They have just finished dinner. The man is looking at the check. He looks worried. Then he puts his hand into his pocket and brings out his wallet. When he looks in his wallet he becomes more upset. What might be the cause for him to be upset?
2. A businessman has just arrived at Los Angeles International Airport. He is waiting at the place where the luggage arrives. He has been waiting for a long time. He still hasn't seen his suitcases. What are some possible reasons he has not been able to find his luggage?
3. A man has just come home from work. He doesn't say hello to his wife. He goes directly into the living room and turns on the TV. His wife looks angry. The man asks his wife, "What's wrong?" "Nothing. Leave me alone," she replies. Why is the woman angry?
4. Professor Jones is writing on the board in front of her class. Suddenly she stops writing. She rests her head on the board for a few minutes. Then she turns and leaves the room very quickly. She doesn't say anything to her students, but closes the door loudly when she leaves the room. Two students who were sleeping in the back of the room wake up and are very surprised that the professor has left. What are some possible reasons for the professor's behavior?
5. You see a man in front of an expensive jewelry store in a large city. He is walking back and forth in front

of the store. He looks into the store when he passes the door. From time to time he looks at his watch. He looks up and down the street nervously. He appears very upset. What are some possible causes for his nervousness?

6. Your roommate has just gone to the mailbox and found a letter for himself. He opens the letter and jumps in the air. He is incredibly happy. He comes into your room and starts to laugh and dance around the room. Why is he so happy?

CHAPTER 15

Endangered Species: Why Are They Endangered?

VOCABULARY PREVIEW   Page 113

A

1. Most animals and plants are adapted to live in a very specific environment.
2. Farmers clear land to grow crops on.
3. We build dams across rivers to produce electricity.
4. Closely related to the destruction of habitats is the pollution of the environment.
5. Another major reason so many species are endangered is the illegal trade in wildlife.
6. Elephant tusks are used to make souvenirs to sell to tourists.
7. Rhinoceroses, or rhinos, are killed for their horns.
8. Some native species face competition from introduced species.

NOTETAKING PREPARATION   Page 114

A

1. So let me quickly repeat for you the first reason that animals are endangered today.
2. I'd like to finish by summing up the main points of today's lecture.
3. Before I go on to my next point, let's review.
4. My lecture today is going to cover the main effects of acid rain.
5. Let's now examine the second reason that elephants are endangered.
6. So before I go, let's review what we have learned this morning.

B

1. Most animals have disappeared from this planet because of natural causes such as climate change.

2. Burning coal and oil can cause acid rain, which results in a great deal of harm to an animal's habitat.
3. Competition for their habitat is a major reason that animals are endangered. This is primarily a direct result of human activity.
4. Humans are also part of the natural world. Therefore, we need to protect plants and animals in order to protect our own future as a species.

FIRST LISTENING   Page 115

Lecturer: Today, I'm going to talk about the reasons why many of the world's plants and animals alive today are in danger of becoming extinct as a result of human activity. The tiger, the mountain gorilla, the rhinoceros, the giant panda—these could all disappear, and many other animals, too. Similarly, many plants are disappearing from the earth. The question is: Why?

Over the centuries, millions of animal and plant species have disappeared. Most of these species disappeared, or became extinct, because of natural causes such as climate changes. Today, however, species are less in danger of becoming extinct because of natural causes. Instead, they are endangered by human activity. OK, let's examine some ways human activity causes plants and animals to become endangered.

The single most important reason why some species are endangered today is the destruction or the pollution of their habitat. Most animals and plants are adapted to live in a very specific environment—the habitat where they live. They cannot survive if they lose the specific habitat that they are adapted to. To give a simple example: a fish lives only under water.

There are many ways that human activity destroys habitats. For example, forests, grasslands, and deserts provide habitats for many plants and animals. We clear these habitats to provide areas for people to live and work in. Farmers clear land to grow crops on. We empty water from wet areas like swamps. We build dams across rivers to provide people with water for farming or to produce electricity. All of these human activities—clearing forests, grasslands, and deserts; emptying swamps; putting dams on rivers—result in the destruction of the specific habitats that many plants and animals need in order to survive.

Closely related to the destruction of habitats is the pollution of the environment, which endangers many species' habitats. Human activity causes air and water pollution from factories, trash, and even farming. This pollution endangers the survival of many animals. Pollution such as oil spills and acid rain harm habitats. You may have seen pictures in newspapers or on TV of dead or dying animals and birds that are covered with oil. This happens after a ship that is transporting oil has an accident that spills the oil into the water. Acid rain that is caused by burning coal and oil also harms many species of fish and many species of trees. Just to sum up, pollution related to human activity such as oil spills and acid rain results in harm to the habitat of many plants and animals.

Another major reason so many species are endangered is the illegal trade in wildlife. Although many governments have passed laws protecting endangered species, animals such as the tiger, the elephant, and the rhinoceros are still hunted illegally. Some people hunt these animals for food, but more often they hunt them only to get specific parts of their bodies, for example, their tusks or their horns. Some endangered species, such as tigers, are illegally hunted for their fur, not for their meat. It's estimated that only about 3,000 wild tigers are left in the world. Elephants, the biggest land animals, are killed for their tusks. The tusks are used to make souvenirs and works of art to sell to tourists and art collectors. Rhinoceroses, or rhinos, are killed for their horns. Rhino horns are used by some people as a medicine, even though studies show the horn doesn't have any medical benefits. Still, in 2010, 333 rhinos were killed illegally in South Africa alone, where three years before only 13 rhinos were killed. Very sad.

OK. The final reason why species are endangered that I'll talk about today is competition for habitat that is a direct result of human activity. As you probably know, animal and plant species have to compete with other animals and plant species in their habitat for food, water, and other resources. This competition is usually not related to human activity. However, some of the competition for habitat *is* directly related to human activity. Some native species face competition from introduced species. These introduced species are plants or animals that are brought, or introduced, by humans into a new habitat, either on purpose or by accident. Let me repeat that: The new species might be introduced *on purpose* or *by accident.*

Take, for example, the rabbits in Australia. The rabbit was not native to Australia. Europeans brought European rabbits to Australia *on purpose* to raise for food, and also a wild rabbit species for hunting. Because of these rabbits, which eat only plants, some native plants became extinct. The habitat of many native animals in Australia was also damaged. The rabbit was introduced on purpose, as I said. The brown tree snake, however, was introduced *by accident* to the island of Guam in the late 1940s. The snakes rode along on military supply planes that landed there. Since then, the brown tree snake has destroyed a large part of the bird population of Guam. So people introduce species on purpose or by accident, and the introduced species harms the native species and habitats.

All right, now, before I finish up this lecture, I'd like to review the three major causes for the increasing number of endangered species today. First, I talked about how human activity is destroying the habitat of many animals. Then I described how illegal wildlife hunting and trading endangers certain species. Finally, I told you how competition from nonnative species introduced into an environment can destroy the native species.

The relationship of all living plants and animals is complex. Each living thing depends on many others. The destruction of one animal or plant species can threaten the survival of other species. We shouldn't forget that human beings are part of the natural world, too, and therefore we need to protect endangered plants and animals so that *we* don't become an endangered species in the future.

SECOND LISTENING   Page 115

Plants and animals alive today are in danger of becoming extinct because of human activity. • The tiger, the mountain gorilla, the rhinoceros, and the giant panda could all disappear. • Similarly, many plants are disappearing from the earth. • The question is: Why? • Over the centuries, millions of animal and plant species have disappeared. • Most of these species disappeared because of natural causes like climate changes. • Today, however, species are less in danger of becoming extinct because of natural causes. • Instead, they are endangered by human activity. • Let's examine some ways human activity causes plants and animals to be endangered. • Some species are endangered today by the destruction or the pollution of their habitat. • Most animals and plants are adapted to live in a very specific habitat. • They cannot survive if they lose the specific habitat that they are adapted to. • A fish lives only under water. • There are many ways that human activity destroys habitats. • Forests, grasslands, and deserts provide habitats for many plants and animals. • Humans destroy these habitats to provide areas for people to live or work in. • Farmers clear land to grow crops on. • We empty water from wet areas like swamps. • We build dams across rivers to provide people with water for farming or electricity. • Clearing forests, grasslands, and deserts result in destruction of habitats. • Filling in swamps and marshes result in destruction of habitats. • Putting dams on rivers result in the destruction of habitats. • Plants and animals need their habitats to survive. • Closely related to the destruction of habitats is the pollution of the environment. • The pollution endangers many species' habitats. • Human activity causes air and water pollution from factories, trash, and even farming. • This pollution endangers the survival of many animals. • Pollution such as oil spills and acid rain harm habitats. • Pictures in newspapers or on TV show dead or dying animals and birds that are covered with oil. • Acid rain harms many species of fish and trees • Another major reason so many species are endangered is the illegal trade in wildlife. • Animals such as the tiger, the elephant, and the rhinoceros are still hunted illegally. • People hunt these animals for food. • People hunt them to get specific parts of their bodies such as tusks or their horns. • Tigers are illegally hunted for their fur, not for their meat. • It's estimated that only about 3,000 wild tigers are left in the world. • Elephants are killed for their tusks to make souvenirs and works of art to sell. • Rhinoceroses, or rhinos, are killed for their horns, to use as a medicine. • Studies show the horn of the rhino doesn't have any medical benefits. • Still in 2010, 333 rhinos were killed illegally in South Africa alone. • Three years before only 13 rhinos were killed. • The final reason species are endangered is competition for habitat caused by humans. • Species have to compete for food, water, and other resources. • This competition is usually not related to human activity. • However, some of the competition for habitat *is* directly related to human activity. • Some native species face competition from introduced species. • These introduced species are brought by humans on purpose or by accident. • *On purpose* or *by accident*! • The rabbit was brought to Australia *on purpose* for food. • A wild rabbit species was introduced for hunting. • Because of these rabbits, which eat only plants, some native plants became extinct. • The habitat of many native animals in Australia was also damaged. • The brown tree snake was introduced *by accident* to the island of Guam in the late 1940s. • The snakes rode along on military supply planes that landed there. • Since then, the brown tree snake has destroyed a large part of the bird population of Guam. • So people introduce species on purpose or by accident. • The introduced species harms the native species and habitats. • I'd like to review the three major causes for the increasing number of endangered species. • First, human activity is destroying the habitat of many animals. • Illegal wildlife hunting and trading endangers certain species. • Competition from introduced species can destroy the native species. • The relationship of all living plants and animals is complex. • The destruction of one animal or plant species can threaten the survival of other species. • We human beings are part of the natural world, too. • We need to protect endangered species. • We need to do this so *we* don't become an endangered species in the future.

THIRD LISTENING   Page 115

Part 1

Lecturer: Today, I'm going to talk about the reasons why many of the world's plants and animals alive today are in danger of becoming extinct as a result of human activity. The tiger, the mountain gorilla, the rhinoceros, the giant panda—these could all disappear, and many other animals, too. Similarly, many plants are disappearing from the earth. The question is: Why?

Over the centuries, millions of animal and plant species have disappeared. Most of these species disappeared, or became extinct, because of natural causes such as climate changes. Today, however, species are less in danger of becoming extinct because of natural causes. Instead, they are endangered by human activity. OK, let's examine some ways human activity causes plants and animals to become endangered.

The single most important reason why some species are endangered today is the destruction or the pollution of their habitat. Most animals and plants are adapted to live in a very specific environment—the habitat where they live. They cannot survive if they lose the specific habitat that they are adapted to. To give a simple example: a fish lives only under water.

There are many ways that human activity destroys habitats. For example, forests, grasslands, and deserts provide habitats for many plants and animals. We clear these habitats to provide areas for people to live and work in. Farmers clear land to grow crops on. We empty water from wet areas like swamps. We build dams across rivers to provide people with water for farming or to produce electricity. All of these human activities—clearing forests, grasslands, and deserts; emptying swamps; putting dams on rivers—result in the destruction of the specific habitats that many plants and animals need in order to survive.

Closely related to the destruction of habitats is the pollution of the environment, which endangers many species' habitats.

Part 2

See First Listening, above.

ACCURACY CHECK   Page 116

1. What is the single most important reason why some species are endangered today?

2. What caused many species to disappear in the past?

3. What happens when a plant or animal species loses its habitat because of human activity?

4. The lecturer mentioned an example of a species that lives only in a specific habitat. What is that species?

5. Give *one* specific example of how humans can endanger the habitats of plants and animals.

6. Give *one* specific example of the pollution of species' habitats by human activity.

7. List *two* examples of an endangered animal.

8. Why are elephants hunted and killed?

9. Why do some people hunt tigers?

10. What are the two reasons rabbits were introduced into Australia by Europeans years ago?

EXPANSION TASK 1 Page 117

The giant panda is found in China. There are two main reasons that it is endangered. First, it is endangered as a result of its habitat destruction. Second, it has been hunted in the past and killed for its fur.

The blue whale is found in all the oceans of the world. It is endangered because it is overhunted, which means "hunted too much." It is hunted partly for its meat and partly for its blubber, which is fat in the whale's body. You can find whale blubber in many different products in the cosmetics industry.

The next animal on the chart that is endangered is the California condor. This is a very large and beautiful bird. It is found in the United States in Southern California and Arizona. It is endangered because its habitat is being destroyed. In some cases it is killed to protect small domestic animals that the condor itself kills for food.

The last animal in our chart is the snow leopard. The snow leopard is found in Central Asia. The snow leopard is overhunted for its fur and is also killed to protect domestic animals on farms and around homes that the leopard might otherwise kill for food for itself.

1. Which endangered animal is found in all the oceans?

2. Which two animals are endangered because they are hunted for their fur?

3. Which two animals are killed to protect domestic animals?

4. Which two animals are endangered because their habitat is being destroyed?

EXPANSION TASK 2 Page 117

1. Waste from factories, humans, animals, agricultural products, and ships leads to this type of pollution. It happens when that waste gets into our rivers and oceans.

2. Some types of human activities damage the earth. Some companies dig into the earth to get out minerals. That causes this type of pollution. Some famers put pesticides on their crops to kill insects. That is another cause of this type of pollution. And when we throw away electronic goods and batteries into our garbage, again this leads to this type of pollution.

3. Traffic, trains, planes, street work, building construction, and loud music all cause this type of pollution. It particularly affects people who live in big cities.

4. This pollution occurs when the atmosphere contains gases, exhaust fumes, smoke, or small pieces of dust. The biggest cause of this type of pollution in cities comes from cars and factories.

5. In many big cities, it is impossible to see the stars at night. People who want to see the stars at night cannot see them because of this type of pollution.

Videoscripts

Surviving an Avalanche

About two months ago, I got caught in a pretty serious avalanche. I went for 2,000 feet. Basically the whole mountainside came down.

When the avalanche happened, I had just finished filming with Jeremy Jones and Xavier de Le Rue in the Tetons. The temperatures were rising pretty significantly so there was a lot of change happening in the snow pack. We were aware of that; you know we've all spent a lot of time in the mountains, and we were trying to manage the terrain and the snow pack. And I was actually third on slope, and those two guys were up on the side on this little safe zone, and I just watched the whole mountain pretty much crack behind me, and I got caught in the avalanche.

I was, you know, probably a few hundred feet down. I was still on top, and I watched a bunch of these trees just snap in half in front of me and went over this big rollover, and I went to the bottom of the snow pack and just got crushed and held down for a while, and then I eventually resurfaced to the top.

You know, when you're at the bottom, you don't want it to stop because you know if it stops, they will never find you 'cause it was too big. So I came up to the top, and eventually you can feel the weight coming off of you. It's really kind of an unbearable amount of weight because it's like hundreds of tons of snow essentially.

And then I came back to the top and I kind of rolled over, and I was back on top of the snow pack. And I looked around me and for a moment, actually, I stopped being scared because just the magnitude of what I was caught in was so incredible that, you know, it was like I had the moment to pause and, you know, you don't generally feel that kind of power ever, especially in an uncontrolled environment.

I remember looking, too, and I looked down and I could see the entire avalanche path, and it was all— I knew I was going to the bottom of the valley and, you know, the trees are like that big and these are like 200, hundred-foot tall trees and I was like, okay, I'm going back to the bott— I'm going all the way and I went another thousand feet to the bottom. And I don't know what happened. I got to the bottom. I could feel it slowing down, and I popped right out at the toe of the avalanche.

You know, it took my partners 20 minutes—30 minutes to even get down, and they were 100 percent sure I was gone. I mean, they would have been less surprised if they had been talking to my ghost. When they showed up and they saw me, they were just— couldn't believe it.

Tristan da Cunha: Oil Spill

Tristan da Cunha—it's the remotest island, remotest inhabited island on earth. And I was lucky enough to travel there this year. Unfortunately, I was also unlucky in that I arrived the same time that a ship wrecked on the island and spilled oil into the water.

And it was devastating. It was a big oil spill that affected a lot of Northern Rock Hopper Penguins, which are already endangered. And so I realized when I landed on this island and saw this, that there was no one else here. Nobody in the world knew about this. There was no communication; there was no way to transmit images.

This is an island that's completely disconnected. It's off the grid, and I happened to land there. So the first thing I did was take as many pictures of this as I could. I created a YouTube video. I published it immediately from the ship, and then I took more pictures and more video. And I Tweeted it. I put it out on Twitter, and it immediately got picked up by the blogosphere.

Now that word is a little outdated, but blogs are important because they're organic. And from this blog—you know we at *National Geographic*, we have an incredible news team—they took my footage, they took my pictures. They published it. They got it out there in the real press, and then this went to the *New York Times*.

But this kind of organic bubbling up of news, of being there, being in the middle of the ocean and capturing these things, this is something that all of you can do and all of you are doing it all the time. When I say, "Be there," I mean be wherever it is that you are. It could be in your own backyard. A lot of you live in Washington, D.C., where things are happening all the time, and believe it or not, you're part of this system where you are reporting.

People, Plants, and Pollinators

Dino Martins: Yes, I am an entomologist, and I know a lot of you think that's strange, but I hope I'll convince you by the end of the fifteen minutes I'm allotted that insects are actually the creatures that do run the world and that are truly, truly wonderful.

But something you may not know is that bees, honeybees, actually originate in East Africa. And just like humans migrated in waves out of Africa, so did honeybees. And the amazing thing with honeybees in Africa is there's a lot of diversity within Africa just like there's a lot of human diversity in Africa. And in East Africa, there are two fantastic varieties of honeybee that we get to work with, the lovely mountain honeybee, Monticola, which is a very gentle chocolate-colored species and produces lots and lots of honey. And then the Savannah or Dryland honeybee, Scutellata, which is not so gentle and not so calm, but also produces lots of honey.

And in addition to honeybees, another social bee that gets managed and that always surprises people to learn about are stingless bees. And Maria here is a beekeeper, a stingless beekeeper, on the slopes of Mount Meru in Tanzania. And you can see a view inside the stingless beehive there. And stingless bee honey—here are two different species of stingless bee honey, Iwele honey and Icore honey, which come from Western Kenya—is as valuable if not more valuable than honeybee honey, which all of these different communities produce.

So I told you a little bit about stingless bees because a lot of the work I'm trying to develop right now is managing and protecting stingless bees. And here is Stanley who is a stingless beekeeper in Western Kenya, at the Kakamega forest, and he keeps five different species of stingless bees. Those are the hives over there. And he even keeps species that scientists don't know about.

Now, bees pollinate crops and wild flowers, and a quick question to you. How many of you like coffee? Chocolate? Yeah. And those are just a couple of examples of two crops that would not exist without the actions of pollinators.

Woman: Today I've learned that there are so many types of bees. I only thought there was only one kind of bee. Today I have found out that there are several kinds of bees. It's so amazing. It's amazing.

Dino Martins: Thank you. And we've found at least 10 different types of bees just here in your shop.

And I have one request to leave you with. If you can spend just five minutes a day in the company of an insect, your life will never be the same again. Thank you.

Free Soloing with Alex Honnold

Jenkins: Free soloing has to be the ultimate in free climbing.

Honnold: It's always a beautiful day to go out soloing.

Jenkins: To free solo is to go without a rope, and to go without gear, to only have your rock shoes and your chalk bag and the power of the mind. It's also very profound. The reason it's probably the ultimate is because one wrong move, you fall, you die.

Honnold: Let me try that again.

Jenkins: And the person at the top of this game, and it's hard to even call this a game, is Alex Honnold. Alex Honnold is probably a perfect example— is someone who has not only trained very hard, but is unbelievably gifted. He is like Michael Jordan.

Honnold: I spend my whole year living in the van traveling from one destination to another. Yeah, I would say that Yosemite probably is the center of my climbing. That all my climbing goals, all training, all kind of revolves around things that I want to do in Yosemite. This is by far my favorite place for soloing because the walls are so inspiring. Like everything here is so big and that's what gets me excited about soloing stuff. One of the most memorable moments was pitch, like, 22 of The Nose. I put my rope away and I switched to just soloing. I just had a moment of, like, this is like surreally cool, I was, like, I can't believe I'm up here with no rope just climbing. Like, this is rad.

Jenkins: Now, Alex has now done the regular route on Half Dome free solo. So, for most people on this planet who are serious climbers, doing Half Dome in a day or two is considered fantastic. Alex did it in three hours, without a rope. He didn't work that route a hundred times, he just got up below it, looked up at it, and believed, absolutely believed, that it was well within his ability.

Honnold: And it seems like in this last season, I've sort of embraced the whole experience, you know, embraced the unpleasant parts, too. It's kind of cool to just look around, you know, enjoy the exposure, and be, like, this is why I'm here. This is awesome.

The Surma People

While we were working on our book, *African Ark*, over a five-year period in Ethiopia, we decided to go into a remote wilderness area in the southwest part of the country. And our goal was to find the Surma people, who live in the southwest, close to the border of Sudan.

There were no roads into the area. We were up and down over ten-thousand-foot mountains and through dense forests of Colobus monkeys, and we finally got to the Surma. And we spent five weeks with this very extraordinary group of people. We were the first white people in that particular area, so initially they were terrified at what had happened and how we had rubbed off our brown skin. And we made very, very close and dear friends. We accompanied them through births—to births, to marriages, to stick fights where they have some of the wildest fights on the continent in order to prove masculinity and win wives.

And at the end of this extraordinary five-week period, where we had really bonded with about 250 of the Surma, we prepared to leave. And the night before we were leaving, we understood that our mule train was going to be ambushed, and that we would not be allowed out alive. And we were extremely disarmed and taken aback by this because we felt we had made such extraordinary bonds with a small group of people in four villages.

And what had happened is, unknowingly, we had broken a cardinal rule of their society. They're an egalitarian people, and we had left out 13,000 other Surma people in establishing our close friendship with three villages. So they felt this was an unacceptable violation of their social system and that we shouldn't be allowed out of Surma land alive. So our guide, Zoga, decided to host a huge gathering of all the elders, and we would have a goat roast. We would have a big feast honoring the chiefs of the Surma.

And at the end of this wonderful day where the chiefs felt really delighted with what had happened, he asked them if they would be willing to escort us out of Surma land and if they'd be willing to get up at 3 a.m. in the morning, which they said, "Of course, we will; it would be our honor."

So at 3:00 a.m. we packed up in the dark, put a chief in between each mule all the way down the line, and headed out in the pitch black of the night with our breath held and our fingers crossed. And by sunrise, we looked up and we saw in the trees the Surma warriors with their Kalashnikovs and AK-47s, pointed at us. But when they saw their chiefs, none of them pulled the trigger. They all just sat there and allowed us to pass out until we got to the border, and we're here to tell the tale.

Images

Inside front cover: Jim Webb/National Geographic Stock, Andrew Evans/National Geographic Stock, Rebecca Hale/National Geogrpahic Creative, Jimmy Chin/National Geographic Stock, Carol Beckwith and Angela Fisher/photokunst, **1:** Laird S. Brown/National Geographic Stock, **2–3:** Leemage/Universal Images Group/Getty Images, **6:** Imagno/Hulton Archive/Getty Images, **7:** Nick Ledger/AWL Images/Getty Images, **8:** C Squared Studios/Photodisc/Getty Images, **9:** Vandeville Eric/ABACA/Newscom, **13:** James L. Stanfield/National Geographic Stock, **15:** Len Langevin/National Geographic Stock, **16:** Peter Macdiarmid/Staff/Getty Images Europe/Getty Images, **22–23:** Tim Laman/National Geographic Stock, **23:** ra photography/E+/Getty Images, **25:** Justin Guariglia/National Geographic Stock, **26–27:** Stela Tasheva/National Geographic My Shot/National Geographic Stock, **30–31:** Robin Smith/Stone Collection/Getty Images, **31:** Lovrencg/Fotolia, **32:** malahova/Fotolia, **32:** malahova/Fotolia, **32:** malahova/Fotolia, **32:** malahova/Fotolia, **32:** malahova/Fotolia, **32:** malahova/Fotolia, **33:** James P. Blair/National Geographic Stock, **37:** Jamie Grill/The Image Bank/Getty Images, **39:** Peter Cade/Iconica/Getty Images, **43:** Yoshikazu Tsuno/AFP/Image Collection, **44:** lightpoet/shutterstock, **44:** lightpoet/shutterstock, **44:** lightpoet/shutterstock, **44:** lightpoet/shutterstock, **44:** lightpoet/shutterstock, **45:** tuja66/fotolia, **45:** Ekaterina Bozhukova/Fotolia, **45:** Viktor/Fotolia, **45:** byggarn.se/Fotolia, **45:** Anson/Fotolia, **46–47:** Andrew Evans/National Geographic Stock, **47:** Kent Kobersteen/National Geographic Stock, **49:** Peter Carlsson/Getty Images, **50:** JIJI Press/Stringer/AFP/Getty Images, **51:** Dennis Macdonald/Photolibrary/Getty Images, **56–57:** Cristina De Paoli/National Geographic My Shot/National Geographic Stock, **60:** Andrew Rodriguez/Fotolia, **63:** Randy Olson/National Geographic Stock, **68:** Michael Melford/National Geographic Stock, **68:** George Grall/National Geographic Stock, **68:** George Grall/National Geographic Stock, **68:** Frans Lanting/National Geographic Stock, **68:** George Grall/National Geographic Stock, **69:** Ralph Lee Hopkins/National Geographic Stock, **69:** George Grall/National Geographic Stock, **69:** George Grall/National Geographic Stock, **69:** Barry Tessman/National Geographic Stock, **69:** Marc Moritsch/National Geographic Stock, **69:** George Grall/National Geographic Stock, **69:** Frans Lanting/National Geographic Stock, **69:** Roy Toft/National Geographic Stock, **70–71:** Amy Toensing/National Geographic Stock, **71:** George Grall/National Geographic Stock, **73:** David Allan Brandt/Iconica/Getty Images, **74–75:** Steve Winter/National Geographic Stock, **79:** Joel Sartore/National Geographic Stock, **79:** Joel Sartore/National Geographic Stock, **80:** picture5479/Fotolia, **81:** Bob Stefko/The Image Bank/Getty Images, **81:** Carl Mydans/Contributor/Time & Life Pictures/Getty Images, **86:** NBC Newswire via Getty Images, **86:** North Wind Picture Archives, **87:** Katherine Young/Hulton Archive/Getty Images, **87:** Maryann Groves/North Wind Picture Archives, **88–89:** Filippo Montefote/AFP/Getty Images, **93:** Archive Holdings Inc./Hulton Archive/Getty Images, **94–95:** Jimmy Chin/National Geographic Stock, **95:** Richard Nowitz/National Geographic Stock, **97:** Ralph Lee Hopkins/National Geographic Stock, **98–99:** Frans Lanting/National Geographic Stock, **104:** Valentin Casarsa/E+/Getty Images, **104:** Mike Powell/Allsport Concepts/Getty Images, **104:** Ross Woodhall/Cultura/Getty Images, **104:** Leland Bobbe/Photonica/Getty Images, **104:** Mitchell Funk/Photographer's Choice/Getty Images, **105:** North Wind Pictures Archives, **110:** Photo_Ma/Fotolia, **110:** Peter Cade/Iconica/Getty Images, **111:** Fuse/Getty Images, **111:** Matthias Tunger/Photographer's Choice RF/Getty Images, **111:** Jochen Tack/arabianEye/Getty Images, **111:** John Lund/Photodisc/Getty Images, **112–113:** Joel Sartore/National Geographic Stock, **117:** Peter Essick/National Geographic Stock, **118–119:** Carol Beckwith and Angela Fisher/photokunst, **119:** Gamma-Rapho via Getty Images